·IRELAND·

PLACES AND PEOPLES OF THE WORLD
IRELAND

J.K. Pomeray

CHELSEA HOUSE PUBLISHERS
New York • Philadelphia

COVER: An ancient stone house falling into disrepair stands guard over rural pasture lands.

Copyright © 1988 by Chelsea House Publishers,
a division of Main Line Book Co.
All rights reserved.

Printed and bound in the United States of America

3 5 7 9 8 6 4 2

Library of Congress Cataloging-in-Publication Data

Pomeray, J. K.
Ireland.

Includes index.

Summary: Surveys the history, topography, people, and culture of Ireland, with emphasis on its current economy, industry, and place in the political world.

I. Ireland—Juvenile literature. [1. Ireland]
I. Title.
DA906.P67   1988   941.5   87-18286

ISBN 1-55546-794-6

Editorial Director: Rebecca Stefoff
Editors: Rafaela Ellis, Bill Finan
Copy Editor: Crystal G. Norris
Series Designer: Anita Noble
Book Designer: A. C. Simon
Map Designer: Maureen McCafferty
Production Manager: Les Kaplan
Production Assistant: K. P. Lane
Photo Research: Marty Baldessari

◄ C O N T E N T S ►

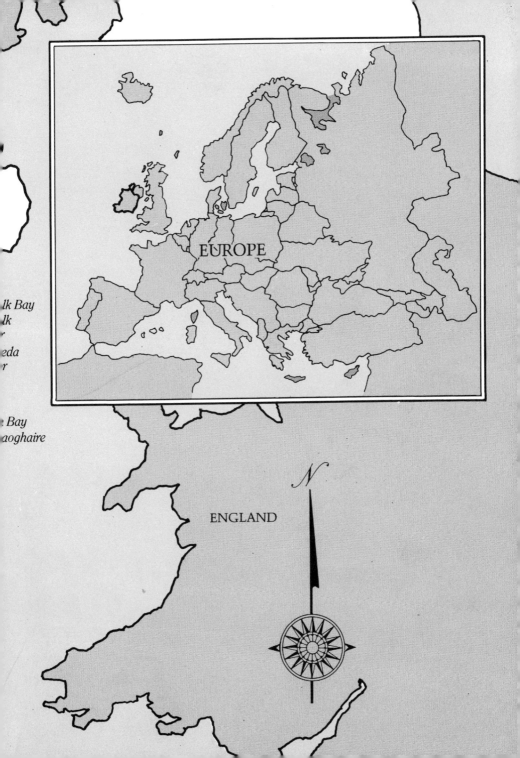

EUROPE

ENGLAND

N

lk Bay
lk
r
eda
r

Bay
aoghaire

◄ FACTS AT A GLANCE ►

Land and People

Area	27,137 square miles (70,556 square kilometers)
Greatest Length	302 miles (486 kilometers)
Greatest Width	171 miles (275 kilometers)
Highest Point	Carrantouhill, 3,414 feet (1,041 meters).
Major Rivers	Shannon, Boyne, Suir, Liffey, Slaney, Barrow, Blackwater, Lee, Nore
Major Lakes	Ree, Mask, Corrib, Derg
Average Annual Temperatures	60° Fahrenheit (15.5° Centigrade), summer; 45° F (7.2° C), winter
Average Annual Rainfall	40 inches (1,016 millimeters)
Population	3,440,427
Population Density	127 people per square mile (49 per sq. km.)
Population Distribution	Rural, 43 percent; urban, 57 percent
Capital	Dublin (population 915,115)
Other Major Cities	Cork (population 149,792), Limerick (population 75,520), Galway (population 41,861), Waterford (population 39,636)
Languages	Gaelic (Irish), English
Literacy Rate	99 percent
Religions	Roman Catholic, 95 percent; Anglican (Church of Ireland), 2.9 percent; Methodist, Presbyterian, and other Protestant, 1 percent; Jewish, 0.06 percent

Holidays	New Year's Day (January 1); St. Patrick's Day (March 17); Good Friday; Easter; Easter Monday; Christmas (December 25); St. Stephen's Day (December 26)

Economy

Agricultural Products	Cattle and dairy products, potatoes, barley, sugar beets, hay, silage (livestock fodder), wheat, sheep, pigs, chickens
Industries	Fishing, food products, automobiles, metals, textiles, chemicals, computers and other electronic equipment, beer, ale, whiskey
Major Imports	Petroleum and petroleum products, road vehicles, electrical machinery, clothing
Major Exports	Meat and meat products, office machines, dairy products, organic chemicals, textiles, live animals
Resources	Zinc, lead, natural gas, barite, copper, gypsum, limestone, dolomite, peat, silver
Gross Domestic Product	U.S. $16.5 billion
Employment	Services, 49.1 percent; industry, 32 percent; agriculture, forestry, and fishing, 18.9 percent
Currency	Irish pound; 0.85 pound equals U.S. $1 or 1 pound equals U.S. $1.18
Average Annual Income	U.S. $4,750

Government

Form of Government	Parliamentary democracy with a president, prime minister, and two houses of Parliament, the Dail and the Seanad
Head of State	President
Head of Government	Prime minister
Eligibility to Vote	All citizens over age 18

◄HISTORY AT A GLANCE►

8000 B.C.	Bands of hunter-gatherers form small settlements along the coastline of Ireland.
4000 B.C.	Irish tribes move inland and begin to farm and raise livestock.
2000 B.C.	The Bronze Age begins in Ireland. Settlers from what are now Spain, Portugal, and France come to the island in search of copper and other minerals. The Irish tribes begin trading with other European peoples.
300s B.C.	The first Celts arrive in Ireland. They quickly become the island's rulers.
around A.D. 300	Much of Ireland is united under the first Celtic high king, who builds the palace at Tara.
390 to 405	Niall of the Nine Hostages rules Ireland.
432	Saint Patrick begins converting the Irish to Christianity.
835	The Vikings invade Ireland, destroying settlements and murdering farmers and monks.
1002	Brian Boru becomes Ireland's first Christian high king.
1014	Brian Boru's forces defeat the Vikings at the Battle of Clontarf, ending the Vikings' hopes of Irish conquest.
1170	Strongbow leads the first wave of Norman invaders at Waterford.
1171	Henry II, king of England, declares himself king of Ireland.

1300s	The Normans control most of Ireland.
1534	British king Henry VIII tries to impose Protestantism on Catholic Ireland.
1553	Queen Mary I begins the "plantation" colonization programs, which deprive Irish clans of their land.
1558	Elizabeth I becomes queen of England and increases persecution of Catholics.
mid-1590s to 1602	The Irish and British clash in the northern part of Ireland.
1607	Most Catholic noblemen of northern Ireland leave the country in the Flight of the Earls.
1603 to 1625	British King James I establishes Ulster Plantation, a settlement for Scottish and English Protestants in northern Ireland.
1641	Irish peasants rise up against British settlers.
1649 to 1652	Oliver Cromwell crushes uprisings and banishes Irish landowners to the western province of Connaught.
1685	James II, a Catholic, assumes the English throne and ends many of the restrictions on Irish Catholics.
1688	The British Parliament takes the crown away from James II and proclaims William of Orange, a Protestant, king.
1690	James II's attempt to regain his crown fails when his troops are defeated at the Battle of the Boyne.
1695	The British enact the Penal Laws, which deprive Irish Catholics of civil rights and religious freedom.
1798	Theobald Wolfe Tone, a Protestant, begins a rebellion against British rule of Ireland. The rebellion fails.
1800	The Act of Union makes Ireland part of Great Britain.
1803	A revolt led by Robert Emmet ends in defeat.
1823 to 1843	Daniel O'Connell, the "Liberator of Ireland," fights for civil rights for Irish Catholics.

1829   The British government passes the Catholic Emancipation Act, which repeals the Penal Laws and allows the Irish to hold elected office.

1845 to 1847   Millions of Irish die when disease destroys the potato crop.

Ships of all nations keep the port of Dublin one of the busiest in Europe.

1858	The Fenian movement, dedicated to Irish independence from England, is founded.
1867	The British crush the Fenian revolt.
1877 to 1891	Charles Stewart Parnell, a Protestant landowner, pushes for Irish home rule. He wins the loyalty of Catholics by defending the rights of tenant farmers.
1886 and 1892	The British Parliament defeats bills calling for Irish home rule.
1893	The Gaelic League is established to promote Irish nationalism.
1905	The independence movement Sinn Fein (Gaelic for "ourselves alone") is founded.
1916	Padraic Henry Pearse leads the Easter Rebellion. It fails, and Pearse and several others are executed.
1918	Seventy-three Irish members of the British Parliament set up the Dail Eireann (House of Deputies) and declare Ireland to be independent. The British refuse to recognize the new government. The rebels form the Irish Republican Army (IRA) to fight a terrorist war. This series of skirmishes becomes known as the Troubles.
1920	The British propose the Government of Ireland Act to split Ireland into two separate political units. The Dail Eireann at first refuses to accept the legislation.
1922	The Government of Ireland Act becomes law and the Irish Free State is founded.
1922	Civil War breaks out between Free Staters and Republicans.
1932	The Fianna Fail party ("warriors of destiny") gains control of the Free State government and begins to sever ties with England.
1937	A new constitution establishes Ireland as a sovereign nation within the British Commonwealth.
1949	Ireland becomes the independent Republic of Ireland.

1955	The Republic of Ireland joins the United Nations.
1973	Ireland joins the European Economic Community.
1970s–1980s	The economy begins to perform poorly. Prices for food, energy, and most other items rise dramatically. Unemployment reaches very high levels. Large numbers of young Irish people emigrate to find better jobs.
late 1980s	Charles Haughey of the Fianna Fail party is prime minister. Economic problems continue.

In the Dark Ages, monks built towers, such as the Ardmore Round Tower in County Waterford, for protection.

Ireland and the World

The long history of the Republic of Ireland is written in stone. It is told by the tombs built by ancient settlers 5,000 to 6,000 years ago; by the early Christian monasteries topped with high round towers to protect the monks from Viking raids; by the great medieval castles built by the Normans; and by the 18th-century estates of wealthy English-Irish landowners.

Ireland's history is also written in tears. Centuries of oppression at the hands of the English continue to haunt the island. The division of the Emerald Isle, as Ireland is known, into two separate nations is the most visible reminder of English rule. The independent Republic of Ireland comprises most of the island's area (26 of its 32 counties). Across a winding border in the northeast lies Northern Ireland, known to the Irish as Ulster. Northern Ireland became a separate territory when Ireland gained independence from Britain in 1922. Today, Northern Ireland is still controlled by Britain. It is the scene of bloody conflict between Catholics and Protestants.

This conflict is rooted in centuries of history—beginning in 1171, when King Henry II of England declared himself king of Ireland. In the centuries that followed, the English gradually seized more and more Irish territory, until they controlled most of the island. When the Protestant Reformation swept Europe in the 16th century, the Protestant English

imposed harsh laws against the Catholic Irish. This religious aspect of the conflict fanned the flames of hatred and mistrust between the two peoples. Ever since, the Irish have viewed their battle against England as a holy war.

Although the Republic of Ireland gained its independence when the island was divided in 1922, the conflict continues. Catholic rebel groups, most notably the Irish Republican Army (IRA), seek to reunite Northern Ireland with the Republic of Ireland. They frequently use terrorism in their

The River Liffey, crossed by thirteen bridges, flows through the center of Dublin.

attempt to make Great Britain give up its claim to Northern Ireland. Protestant extremist groups counter with terrorism of their own. As a result, Northern Ireland has become divided along religious lines in a civil war that shows no signs of ending. Although life in the Republic of Ireland is more peaceful, most citizens of the Republic are greatly disturbed by the war in the north.

Ireland's people have contributed much to the progress of mankind. While mainland Europe was nearly overwhelmed by barbarism during the

A young Irish boy points to the signs of continuing conflict—bullet holes made when his babysitter was shot when she answered a knock on the door.

Dark Ages (from the 6th century to the 9th), Christian monks and priests led a golden age of learning and art in Ireland. In later centuries, when Irish leaders were forced into exile by conquest and oppression, many gave distinguished service to the lands they adopted as new homes—lands that included France, Spain, Austria, and countries in North and South America. Irish people have led many other movements for liberty in addition to their own, and they have fought for the poor and downtrodden throughout the world. Millions of Irish immigrants literally helped lay the foundations of much of our world today, building cities, roads, railways, harbors, canals, power stations, and factories on three continents. And, last but not least, the world of art—painting, sculpture, music, and especially literature—has been immeasurably enriched by the works of Irish artists.

The Republic of Ireland is a land rich in tradition and respect for the past. But it is also a land full of hopes for the future. Its ideals are perhaps best embodied by its flag, introduced by Thomas Meagher in 1848. The flag has three colored bands of equal size. The green band represents Ireland's original Celts and their descendants, the Catholics. The orange band represents the island's Protestant tradition. And the white band in the middle symbolizes the hope of truce and unification between the two.

The cliffs at Kinsale Head in County Cork are but one example of Ireland's beautiful coastline.

The Emerald Isle

The tiny island of Ireland lies on the European continent's western fringe. Sometimes called "Europe's last outpost," it is bounded by the Atlantic Ocean on the south, west and northwest and by the North Channel on the northeast. To the east, the Irish Sea separates Ireland from Great Britain—England, Scotland, and Wales. Once a single nation, Ireland is divided into two countries today. The Republic of Ireland, the subject of this book, makes up most of the island—about 83 percent, or 27,137 square miles (70,556 square kilometers).

About 10,000 years ago, Ireland was part of the European mainland. But as the Ice Age ended and the great glaciers melted, the seas rose, cutting off the island from the rest of Europe. The receding glaciers left behind a great quantity of rock and a rich layer of soil that divide Ireland into two geographic areas: the coastal highlands and the central plain.

The coastal highlands form a rough ring around the island. The highlands are a series of low mountain ranges, including the Wicklow, Knockmealdown, Comeragh, Kerry, Connemara, Mayo, and Donegal mountains. Ireland's highest point, Carrantuohill, located west of Killarney in an area known as Macgillicuddy's Reeks, rises a mere 3,414 feet (1,041 meters) above sea level, and only a few other peaks reach 3,000 feet (900 m). But what Ireland's mountains lack in height, they make up for in beauty. Many centuries of erosion have given them a gentle, rounded appearance that lends a sense of peacefulness and timelessness to the Irish landscape. As an old Irish proverb says, "The people go, but the hills remain."

Inland from the coastal highlands lies the central plain, a land of green, gently rolling meadows. Only a few scattered trees and rocks (natural formations and man-made boundary walls) break up the pastoral landscape. This is farm country, where fertile soil and a mild climate allow farmers to grow fine crops and raise high-quality livestock. Because the average altitude of the central plains is only 300 feet (90 m) above sea level, heavy rains sometimes cause floods in the low-lying areas.

Coastline, Lakes, and Rivers

Although Ireland is only about 300 miles (480 kilometers) long and 171 miles (275 km) wide, it has 1,969 miles (3,170 km) of seacoast. Much of this is rough and rocky, with many bays and inlets. The deep bays on the western coast—including Galway, Sligo, Donegal, Clew, Tralee, Dingle,

Killarney is one of the world's outstanding beauty spots. Every feature of the district's landscape is associated with some legend of the past.

and Bantry—provide excellent natural harbors for fishing and merchant vessels. The south coast also has several good deep-water harbors, notably Cork Harbor, where the River Lee meets the Atlantic Ocean, and Waterford, at the mouth of the River Suir. Principal east coast harbors include Wexford on Wexford Bay, Dun Laoghaire on Dublin Bay, Dublin Harbor at the mouth of the River Liffey, Dundalk on Dundalk Bay, and Drogheda at the mouth of the River Boyne.

Dozens of small, windswept islands lie off the coast to the west and southwest. These include Achill Island, Clare Island, Valencia Island, and the Aran Islands, a popular tourist area.

Ireland has a number of sparkling blue lakes, known as loughs (pronounced locks). Most are located in the central or western counties. Among the most scenic are Lough Mask and Lough Corrib in County Galway, Lough Conn in County Mayo, and the three small loughs of Killarney in County Kerry. Others include Lough Ree and Lough Derg along the River Shannon, Lough Melvin on the Northern Ireland border, and Lough Allen in County Leitrim.

Many beautiful rivers wind their way through Ireland. The Shannon, Ireland's longest river, starts in County Cavan in the northern part of the republic and flows for about 240 miles (386 km) before emptying into the Atlantic Ocean between the southwest counties of Munster and Clare. Other important rivers include the Barrow, the Blackwater, the Boyne, the Slaney, the Moy, the Nore, the Suir, the Lee, and the Liffey. Dublin, Ireland's largest city, is divided into two sections by the River Liffey. Cork, the second-largest city, was founded on an island in the River Lee.

Climate

Ireland's weather is often summed up in two words: wet and mild. Although the island has a latitude corresponding to that of Canada's icy Labrador peninsula, its weather is surprisingly warm and changes little through the year. Temperatures average about 60° Fahrenheit (15.5° Centigrade) in the summer and 45° F (7.2° C) in the winter; snow is rare.

Ireland's mild climate is due in large part to its location in the path of the Gulf Stream, a massive Atlantic Ocean current that travels from south of the Equator to the northern reaches of the ocean. The Gulf Stream's warm water helps keep temperatures mild. The warm air that accompanies the current creates clouds, rain, and the fabled Irish mist when it meets the cold winds of the North Atlantic.

Annual rainfall averages about 40 inches (1,016 millimeters), distributed fairly evenly throughout the year. The western part of the island

Houses at Slea Head in County Kerry command an impressive view of the sea.

receives slightly more rainfall than other areas. The combination of mild temperatures and steady rainfall keeps Ireland green year round, accounting for its nickname, the "Emerald Isle."

Natural Resources

Ireland has always suffered from a lack of fuel and mineral resources. Its supply of gold was rapidly used up in ancient times, when Irish ornaments made of the precious metal were widely traded throughout continental

Europe. Resources such as oil, coal, iron, tin, and other metals have had to be imported. Ireland does have small natural deposits of coal and copper, but these are hard to mine. They are mined only in times of great world demand, when prices are high. In recent decades, modern exploration and mining methods have yielded some unsuspected mineral riches, including lead and other minerals in County Galway and silver from reopened mines in County Tipperary.

Peat bogs are expected to provide fuel for the next 100 years. About 15 percent of Ireland is covered by such bogs.

Even more recently, deposits of natural gas and oil—two important modern fuels—have been discovered in several places off Ireland's coast. Some of the natural gas is already being used in Ireland, and the Irish government is encouraging the development of large-scale oil production.

Ireland's most important natural resource is its traditional source of fuel—peat, sometimes called turf. Peat is highly compressed vegetation, mostly mosses and grasses, that is thousands of years old. It forms in bogs—wet, low-lying areas that are scattered over many parts of the island, especially in the central plains and the western counties.

When peat is dried, it makes a very good fuel. People throughout rural Ireland use peat for heating and cooking, and some large power stations burn it to generate electricity for Ireland's towns and cities.

Country people still harvest and dry peat as their ancestors did centuries ago. Using a special shovel called a *slean*, they cut the peat into rectangular bricks about the size of small fireplace logs. Then, they drain the water out of the bricks, stack them in small tripods (a process known as "footing the turf"), and leave them in the sun to dry. Once the bricks are dry, the villagers load them onto a donkey or small horse, which carries them over the bogs to the roadside. (The animals are used because wheeled vehicles would get stuck in the swampy bogs.)

The rural Irish keep their peat bricks in exposed piles or small sheds near their house. They burn the bricks in fireplaces and stoves, much as wood is burned in other parts of the world. On chilly nights, a warm peat fire becomes the central gathering place for many rural Irish families.

Modern methods of collecting and drying peat have made it more efficient as a fuel for power stations. One new method is the use of harvesting machines that "float" on a bog's surface. Some of these machines crush the peat and form it into cakes, which are allowed to dry in the sun; others crumble it into milled peat, a dust that can be blown through huge furnaces and burned in power-generating stations.

Scientists expect Ireland's peat bogs to provide fuel for the next 100 years. About 15 percent of the nation is covered by bogs; in many western coastal areas, "blanket bogs" make thousands of acres of land uninhabitable. But the land was not always bog-covered. Ancient tools and other traces of Stone Age settlements found in these bogs suggest that the area was once fertile, but that it slowly changed over thousands of years. Methods are now being developed to make cleared bogs productive for farming and forestry.

Ireland's other important natural resource is its fertile soil. Two-thirds of the country, mostly in the central plains, is still devoted to farmland. Rich grasses cover most of the plains, allowing ranchers to raise livestock, Ireland's most important agricultural product.

Ireland's deposits of rock and stone include limestone, granite, and marble. Many people believe that the rich limestone base of the soil in the Curragh, an area of County Kildare, provides ideal pastureland for grazing race horses, and many of the world's champion horses come from this region. But Irish stone has been most important for building. It is displayed in structures all over the island, from prehistoric tombs to 18th-century cathedrals.

Because of its isolation and small size, Ireland has only a limited variety of plant and animal life when compared with mainland Europe and even Great Britain. Ireland's native wildlife population is sparse. The last wolf was reportedly killed in 1786. The only reminder of the long-extinct Irish elk that once roamed the central plains are the 8-foot (2.4-meter) antlers occasionally found preserved in peat bogs. The largest native wild animals remaining on the island are foxes, otters, badgers, and red deer. Some animals that are not native to the island, including the rabbit and the brown rat, have thrived there since they were introduced centuries ago.

The waters that surround the Irish isle are rich in sea life. Herring, cod, salmon, mackerel, and lobster abound. The coasts also serve as a habitat for many varieties of seabirds.

Most of the island's original forests were cleared long ago, when Ireland was under British rule. The forests had been so extensively cut for building materials and fuel by the 18th century that an Irish poet wondered, "What shall we do for timber? The last of the woods is down." Little native forestland remains today, but many upland bogs are being planted with fast-growing trees, such as pines, that will provide a valuable source of building materials and paper.

Despite the lack of forestland, Ireland is lush and green with a variety of grasses, mosses, ferns, and flowering plants. Its national flower is the shamrock, a flowering three-leaf clover.

Warring tribes of the Bronze Age built many forts. This is the entrance to Staigue Fort in County Kerry.

Early History

Many traditional Irish poems, songs, and stories tell of the glorious days before English domination. They are about magical heros—Finn Mac-Cool, Brian Boru, Cuchulainn. These old folktales, still told and sung today, relate the story of Ireland in the years before written history. They also provide a window into the Irish character, the curious mixture of tragedy and comedy, tears and laughter, that is so typical of the spirit of Ireland and its people.

Most of these tales end tragically in death and defeat, and in many ways, Ireland's story is a tragedy, a long history of struggles. For centuries, the Irish people were independent; then, in the 12th century, they were conquered by England. Finally independent again in the 20th century, they have been divided into two separate nations, and those in Northern Ireland must endure a bitter conflict that rages to this day.

Prehistoric Ireland

Ireland's story begins long before recorded history. Archaeological evidence suggests that human beings first came to Ireland about 10,000 years ago, in an era known as the Mesolithic Period, or Middle Stone Age. Ireland was one of the last areas of Europe to become inhabited. Thousands of years before, while most of Ireland was still covered by the glaciers of the Great Ice Age, prehistoric human beings were already living in caves in what are now France and Spain.

Ireland's first inhabitants probably traveled across the land bridges that once connected the island with what is now Scotland—land bridges that later were submerged as the great glaciers melted and the seas rose. These first inhabitants lived in small tribal settlements near the coastline, mainly along the eastern and northern shores. They survived by gathering berries and shellfish, and they made crude stone tools. Some of these tools, along with ancient piles of shells and other evidence of human life, have been unearthed and dated by archaeologists.

By the time of the Neolithic Period, or Late Stone Age—about 6,000 years ago—the Irish tribes had begun to farm and raise livestock. Slowly, they moved inland from the coasts to establish settlements. Many relics of this era have been found, including pieces of pottery, fairly advanced stone tools and weapons, and even the remains of wooden buildings. In the 1960s, a wooden house dating back some 5,200 years was unearthed near Cookstown in Northern Ireland.

The most striking relics left behind by these ancient people are their stone tombs. Hundreds of these tombs have been found throughout Ireland, including about 300 of a type known as passage graves. Usually located on a hilltop, a passage grave consists of a large mound of dirt or stone (known as a cairn) that conceals a stone burial chamber inside. A stone passageway leads to the burial chamber, which may have several rooms. Because these stone tombs are similar to the tombs of other ancient peoples who lived in Great Britain and the European mainland, many archaeologists believe that people sailed to Ireland from these areas in the Late Stone Age.

The most famous passage grave of all is Newgrange in County Meath. It is considered one of the finest prehistoric relics in all of Europe. This grave is still covered by much of its original 50,000-ton stone cairn (a cairn is a man-made heap of stones). It extends over almost a full acre of ground and has an entrance passage that is 60 feet (18 meters) long and decorated with many carved stones. The central burial chamber is 20 feet (6 m) high; three side chambers open out from the central chamber. They contain stone basins that probably were used in some sort of ancient burial rite (the grave's other contents have long since been removed). Another famous passage grave is Queen Maeve's Cairn, on Knocknarea in County Sligo. Unlike most of the others, this grave has never been opened.

Other Stone Age monuments found in the Irish countryside include large standing stones, some of which apparently served as grave markers. Others are believed to have been boundary indicators or ritual objects. Some of them are inscribed with *ogham*—a primitive system of writing consisting of simple strokes.

Around 2,000 B.C., the Stone Age in Ireland gave way to the Bronze Age as people learned how to make instruments from metal. Far superior to stone tools, metal tools and weapons enabled the people to farm better and to expand their settlements. Metal also brought more people to the island from mainland Europe, because settlers sailed from what are now Spain, Portugal, and France in search of copper and other minerals. These people brought their native crafts and designs, which skilled Irish artisans developed into high art. Irish ornaments, especially the distinctive lunulae (crescents of thin gold, finely engraved with intricate geometric patterns), were prized throughout Europe. Irish weaponry was also highly

This Stone Age implement, made of chipped flint, was found with the bones and tooth of an elephant.

In this early Celtic religious ceremony, Druids (or priests) are sacrificing a bull.

valued. Goods from as far away as the Mediterranean were traded for Irish swords and other weapons.

As the Bronze Age continued and Ireland's tribes grew in size and in power, weapons became more and more important. By 500 B.C., fighting between tribes was commonplace. Irish museums are filled with daggers, swords, and axes from this period. Other evidence of these tribal wars includes several Bronze Age forts. These forts fall into two distinct categories: hill forts (such as Haven Fort near Armagh in Northern Ireland), which were built on mounds and surrounded by ditches; and ring forts (including the Crannogand ring fort recently restored near Kilmurray), in which walls were created by weaving thick branches through heavy upright stakes set in a circle.

During this period, the first Celts came to Ireland from Great Britain and western Europe. Their arrival marked the start of the Iron Age in Ireland. It also marked the beginning of a civilization that would endure more than 1,500 years and a language that is still spoken today.

Celtic Ireland

The Celts (or Gaels, as they are often called in Ireland) were a bold, warlike people who originated in the area that is now Germany. Around 500 B.C., they began to spread out from their homelands in the northern Alps and along the Danube River, moving in all directions throughout Europe. They settled in much of what was then the Roman Empire: Gaul (France), northern Italy, and the Spanish peninsula. Although the early Celts left no recorded history of their own, Roman writers of the time described them as a lively, imaginative people fond of fighting and hunting as well as poetry and storytelling. They had a complex tribal society made up of chieftains, warriors, poets, and Druids (the priests of their mystical religion).

Along with other Germanic tribes such as the Anglo-Saxons and the Franks, the Celts were in constant conflict with the Roman Empire. Shortly before 400 B.C., an army of Celts marched into southern Italy. In 390 B.C., under their leader, Brennus, they defeated a large Roman army and sacked the city of Rome. Gradually, however, the Romans pushed the Celts and other Germanic tribes back into central and western Europe.

Under Roman pressure, the Celts moved farther west into Gaul and then crossed the sea into Great Britain. Eventually, in about the 4th century B.C., they entered Ireland. The circumstances surrounding their arrival are unclear, but we do know that the Celts quickly dominated the ancient Irish tribes and became masters of the island. They may have triumphed because of superior iron weaponry and fighting skills or simply greater numbers. The original people remained in most parts of Ireland, however, and were able to retain many of their customs under Celtic rule.

In Ireland, the Celts were finally free of Roman influence. Although Roman armies had reached Great Britain, they did not follow the Celts to Ireland. Left alone to rule the island, the Celts developed a unique social system. Celtic priests and judges, and the poets and storytellers who preserved the Celts' unwritten history, formed a prestigious learned class, which was considered sacred. Warriors became the nobility, and the native Irish became nothing more than their slaves.

Society was regulated by a complex system of rules known as the Brehon Laws (named for Celtic judges known as *brehons*). These laws determined everything from the proper succession of kings to the details of domestic life. Many of these laws endured into the 1500s, and they are the basis of the country's present justice system.

Although they had a highly organized, rigid social system, the Celts developed no real political unity for centuries. They had a natural fondness for warfare, and disputes among the various families, or clans, were usually settled on a battlefield. As a result, the island was divided into many individual kingdoms, each known as a *tuath*. At one point, as many as 150 tuatha (the plural of tuath) divided Ireland. Each was ruled by a Celtic king, or *ri*. Sometimes, several tuatha were combined into a larger unit known as a *mor-tuath*, which was ruled by a more powerful ri.

Sometime around the 3rd century A.D., much of Ireland was united under a single *ard ri*, or high king. The high king built a magnificent palace on the Hill of Tara over looking the river Boyne. Tara became the first real capital of Ireland; from his palace there, the high king issued decrees, settled disputes, and presided over festivals that usually included several days of games and contests of music-making and storytelling. One important high king of this period was Niall of the Nine Hostages, who ruled from A.D. 390 to 405. According to legend, Niall built five roads throughout Ireland, all of which led to Tara.

Today, hardly a trace of these roads or the palace of Tara remains. But the Celtic language, now called Gaelic or Irish, has survived. People throughout Ireland, especially in the western counties, still speak Gaelic, although their numbers are dwindling. In fact, the Irish refer to their country as "Eire" or "Erin," names that come from the Celtic word Eriu, the name of an ancient goddess.

Because the Celts did not have a written language (except for the primitive ogham lettering used on graves and standing stones), their history was passed down orally from generation to generation. As the stories were made more colorful by each new generation of storytellers, they took on the quality of legend. Many of these stories are still told today.

The warrior Cuchulainn is an important figure in many early Celtic stories. He is described as a man of great size and strength, with seven fingers on each hand, seven toes on each foot, and seven pupils in each eye. Cuchulainn's most famous exploit was single-handedly defending Ulster (a province in northern Ireland) from an entire army.

Later stories tell of Finn MacCool, another Irish hero. Finn led a band of young warriors, known as the Fianna, who served the legendary high king Cormac Mac Art. To become a member of the Fianna, a candidate had to be able to leap over tree branches as high as his head and run under branches no higher than his knees without disturbing a leaf or a twig, and to pick a thorn out of his foot while running at top speed. He also had to be able to recite many old poems and stories.

The Coming of Christianity

Toward the end of the 3rd century, the Roman Empire declined. The Celts began raiding Roman subjects in Britain and trading with people on the European mainland. As the Celts had more contact with the outside world, Christianity began to make its way across the sea to Ireland. Although the Irish people practiced a religion known as Druidism (a type of nature worship), Christianity soon took hold.

The first official recognition of Christianity in Ireland is thought to have occurred in 431, when the Pope appointed a bishop named Palladius "to the Irish believing in Christ." But Christianity did not spread throughout the island until a man named Patrick became Ireland's bishop. Later known as Saint Patrick, he gets the credit for bringing Christianity to Ireland.

Patrick was born somewhere in Britain around 390. His parents were Christians and Roman subjects. When Patrick was 16, a Celtic raiding party sent out by Niall of the Nine Hostages captured him and some other Roman subjects and brought them back to Ireland to serve as slaves. For six years, Patrick tended sheep in a remote part of northern Ireland. During this time, he became deeply committed to Christianity.

Eventually, Patrick fled Ireland and returned home. He then made his way to France, where he studied to be a priest. He was ordained in about

St. Patrick, the patron saint of Ireland, converted the Celts to Christianity.

417 and spent the next 15 years at Auxerre, a city in northeastern France. Ireland's bishop, Palladius, died in 431, and Pope Celestine I sent Patrick to take his place the following year. Patrick traveled throughout the island, teaching the people about Jesus Christ and encouraging them to give up Druidism.

Within 30 years, Patrick had succeeded in converting most of the Irish to Christianity. With the help of missionaries from Britain and France, he established a national church, based in Armagh. Patrick is thought to have established more than 300 churches throughout Ireland, and personally to have baptized more than 100,000 people. He also taught many people to read Latin so that they could study the Bible on their own.

Today, Patrick is Ireland's patron saint. The day of his death—March 17—is an Irish national holiday, known as Saint Patrick's Day. All over the world, people of Irish descent celebrate March 17 in honor of the man who converted the Celts.

The Celts' acceptance of Christianity quickly changed the whole character of Ireland. It ushered in a golden age of learning in the many monasteries that sprang up throughout the countryside. In these sanctuaries, devout monks studied and taught everything from Christian doctrine to art, science, and mathematics. (Although most monastics were men, some were women. Saint Brigid was an Irish woman who founded a religious community known as the Church of the Oak on the banks of the River Liffey at Kildare.)

Christianity also brought written language to Ireland. The monks wrote many volumes in Latin and soon developed a written Gaelic language to record the Celtic legends. They toiled long hours to create manuscripts of exquisite beauty, with multicolored designs and graceful lettering. The finest examples of this style, known as illuminated manuscripts, are considered artistic masterpieces.

The most beautiful of the illuminated manuscripts is the Book of Kells. Completed in the 8th century by Irish monks, the manuscript contains passages from the Bible's New Testament as well as portraits of Christ and the Apostles. It is decorated with illustrations of incredible complexity and detail. Giraldus of Wales, a 12th-century visitor to Ireland, described the book. "If you look closely," he wrote, "you will notice such intricacies, so delicate and subtle, so close together and well-knitted, so and bound together, and so fresh still in their coloring that you hesitate to declare that these things must have been the result of k, not of men, but of angels." Today, the Book of Kells is kept in Trinity College Library in Dublin.

In addition to manuscripts and scholarship, Ireland's early monks left behind some stunning architecture. Some monks chose to live as hermits (either alone or in small groups), and they built monasteries in remote areas, such as the mountain valleys and the rocky islands off the Atlantic coast. One of these settlements is located on Great Skellig, a barren rock island off the southwestern coast. It can be reached only by climbing a steep flight of rock steps that stretches some 600 feet (180 m) above the sea. At the top of the steps stands a group of stone churches and round huts, along with the remains of a graveyard, a well, and a few garden terraces. More than 1,000 years after it was abandoned, the monastery remains in almost perfect condition.

The Dark Ages

From the fall of the Roman Empire at the end of the 5th century until the start of the Middle Ages in about the 10th century, Europe experienced a period often called the Dark Ages. During this time of great upheaval, Germanic tribes overran the crumbling Roman Empire. While these so-called "barbarians" struggled to create a culture of their own, much of the knowledge and art of the Greeks and Romans was forgotten.

But in their island isolation, Irish monks kept the light of knowledge alive during this period, and Ireland enjoyed what some now call its golden age of learning and art. Yet while the arts flourished, political disintegration began. After the death of Niall of the Nine Hostages, no strong central ruler emerged. The high king at Tara became little more than a figurehead. Independent kings fought among themselves and frequently defied him.

By the 9th century, towns were growing and governments were becoming centralized throughout Europe. But in Ireland, most of the peo-

Around 835 A.D., the Vikings burst out of Norway and raided much of western Europe, including Ireland.

ple still lived in scattered tribal settlements. Because of this, the Irish were totally unprepared to resist any challenge to their way of life. They faced such a challenge in the 9th century, when the warlike Vikings invaded the Emerald Isle.

The Vikings were daring, seafaring warriors from Scandinavia (the area that is now Norway, Sweden, and Denmark). Starting in the 8th century, Viking raiders left their homeland to terrorize the coasts and waterways of Europe. Their sleek, fast ships enabled them to sail great distances in search of new places to plunder.

Around 835, the Vikings reached the shores of Ireland. In its state of political disunity, Ireland had no organized force to withstand the raiders. Up and down the coasts and along the big rivers, the Vikings stole cattle, destroyed settlements, and murdered farmers. The pagan invaders also sacked the monasteries, stealing valuable artwork and religious relics and slaughtering the pious monks.

In an effort to protect themselves and their treasures, the monks built tall, round towers of stone. Some of these were over 100 feet (30 m) high. All had thick walls and a single door high off the ground that could be reached only by a tall ladder. Inside were wooden floors and stairways and a few narrow windows to provide light. Several of these towers remain standing today in the Irish countryside.

Soon after arriving in Ireland, the Vikings began to establish their own settlements along the coast. They founded the first Irish towns, including Dublin, Wexford, Waterford, Wicklow, and Limerick. These towns began to change the character of society in Ireland. Before the Vikings arrived, Irish society had been rural, with no real towns. Livestock had been the main measure of wealth and status; Celtic chiefs even collected taxes in the form of cattle and horses. But the Vikings introduced money to Ireland. They traded the gold seized from the monasteries for luxury goods from abroad; soon, imported jewelry, silks, wines, and other goods became the standards of wealth. Because the coastal towns were the centers of this rich trade, people flocked to them.

Eventually, Viking men began to marry Irish women, and the two cultures started to blend. (In fact, many contemporary Irish names, such as Doyle and Loughlan, are of Scandinavian origin.) Viking warriors often intervened in disputes between local Irish chiefs; for example, the kings of Leinster once got help from the Vikings of Dublin in their struggle with the neighboring province of Meath. From the Vikings, the Irish learned the art of trading. At the same time, many Vikings adopted Christianity. They built several Christian cathedrals, including the famous Christ Church Cathedral that still stands in Dublin.

By the end of the 10th century, the Vikings were at the height of their power. They controlled great areas of Ireland. The native Irish, with no strong leader to rally them, could do little to resist. But in the year 1002, Brian Boru became high king of Ireland.

Considered the first true Irish statesman, Brian brought much-needed unity to the Irish people. He viewed Ireland as a single nation rather than a collection of independent kingdoms, and began to centralize the Irish government and church. He also attempted to organize Irish society. Under his guidance, the Irish became one of the first peoples to adopt hereditary surnames. Most of these names used the prefix "O'" or "Mac," meaning son or descendant of. For example, Brian's own family became known as O'Brian. A devout Christian, Brian helped restore the monasteries and churches that the early Vikings had destroyed. He also built roads and forts and began to gather a strong army.

But Brian married a woman named Gormflath, who proved to be as treacherous as she was beautiful. Along with Sitric, her half-Viking son from a previous marriage, and Maelmora, her brother, Gormflath plotted an uprising against Brian. With Sigurd the Stout, a Viking leader who had been frustrated in his attempts to conquer Scotland, she made a deal: she would marry him if he would aid in her plot against Brian. Seeing his chance to gain a foothold in Ireland, Sigurd agreed. He sent his warriors to join with the forces already assembled by Sitric, who was the leader of Dublin, and Maelmora, the provincial king of Leinster.

Although Brian was by this time an old man of 74, he was ready to meet the challenge. On Good Friday 1014, he marched his army from his headquarters at Kincora on the River Shannon to the field of Clontarf, just north of Dublin, where the Viking troops waited. Although Brian wanted to lead the troops into battle himself, his eldest son persuaded him to stay behind in his tent. A fierce, bloody battle raged from sunrise to sunset. When it was over, 7,000 Vikings and 4,000 Irishmen lay dead or dying. Brian's troops emerged victorious—but as the beaten Vikings fled the battlefield, one of them overpowered Brian's guards, entered the tent, and killed him.

Today, Brian Boru is honored as one of Ireland's greatest heroes. He not only began to unite the Irish people but forever dashed the Vikings' hopes of conquering all of Ireland.

The Normans

Although the Irish had defeated the Vikings in the Battle of Clontarf, Brian Boru's death left them once again without a strong leader. As a result, although they were undisturbed by outsiders for the next 150 years,

King Brian Boru (926–1014) met his death at the hands of the invading Vikings.

they fought constantly among themselves. In addition to this political unrest, there was also religious turmoil. The Irish church was disorganized. Although the island had several important monasteries, the individualistic monks were becoming more and more distanced from the central authority of the Pope in Rome.

Into this confusion came the Normans, the descendants of Viking settlers in France. These hardened conquerors had landed in England in 1066 and had completely overrun it by the end of the century. In the 12th century, England's Norman king, Henry II (also called Henry Plantagenet), asked for and received Pope Adrian IV's permission to move into Ireland and bring the Irish monks back into line with Rome.

Henry's motives for conquest were not only religious, however. He was eager to expand his territory and had coveted the rich Irish lands for some time. He saw his chance in 1170, when Dermot MacMurrough, king of Leinster Province, invited Norman troops to help in his struggle with Irish high king Rory O'Connor. In August of that year, a Norman force led by Richard de Clare, Earl of Pembroke—also known as Strongbow— landed at Waterford on the southeastern coast of Leinster.

King Rory's forces were no match for Strongbow's experienced and highly disciplined fighters. The Normans were armed with the most modern weapons of the age, including crossbows and longbows, which could fire arrows more than 100 yards (91 m) with deadly accuracy. They were clad in heavy, chain mail armor for protection. The Irish, on the other hand, wore only linen tunics and were equipped mainly with swords, spears, and axes.

Strongbow and his men quickly took Waterford and Dublin. In gratitude, King Dermot gave his daughter, Eva, in marriage to Strongbow, and promised that their children would succeed to the kingship of Leinster. But when Dermot died, Strongbow himself assumed the throne.

Strongbow's men encouraged him to break away from England's King Henry and form an independent Norman empire in Ireland. Worried that Strongbow was gaining too much power, Henry came to Ireland in 1171 with an army of more than 4,000 soldiers and 500 knights. He was welcomed by the church and after obtaining Strongbow's pledge of loyalty, he declared himself king of Ireland. Ignoring Rory O'Connor, the high king, Henry divided Irish lands among his own nobles and the few Irish provincial kings in the south and east who submitted to his authority.

The Irish chieftains were powerless to prevent the seizure of their territories. By the 1300s, the Normans controlled almost all of the island. They strengthened their hold by building castles, first of wood and then of stone. These stone castles include Limerick Castle in the city of Limerick, Kilkenny Castle and Granagh Castle in County Kilkenny, Mallow Castle in County Cork, Roscommon Castle and Ballintober Castle in County Roscommon, and Trim Castle in County Meath. A Gaelic poem of the time describes the building of Trim Castle:

> Then Hugh de Lacy
> Fortified a house at Trim
> And threw a fosse [trench] around it
> And then enclosed it with a herisson [stockade].
> Within the house he then placed
> Brave knights of great worth.

The land around these castles was divided along feudal lines into parcels known as baronies. The Norman noblemen who were granted these baronies ruled them almost as kings, with their own armies and courts.

Although the English (as the Normans were known by the 13th century) controlled Ireland, they were not successful in controlling its people. The English king forbade the noblemen to set up an independent government in Ireland, and the enforcement of English law was often impossible in Ireland's remote areas. The Irish clansmen who still held many areas of the countryside constantly clashed with English soldiers outside the castle walls.

The cross-bow was introduced into Irish warfare by Norman mercenaries. This painting depicts an Irish cross-bowman with his weapon, sometimes called an arbalest.

As a result of their isolation from England and English authority, the English settlers in the Irish countryside developed a strong sense of independence. They began to intermarry with the Irish and to adopt their Gaelic language and way of life. As an old saying goes, they became "more Irish than the Irish themselves."

England saw this as a threat to its control of Ireland and took steps to stop the settlers from mingling with the native people. When the first Irish Parliament was formed late in the 13th century, only Englishmen were allowed to be members, and discussions were conducted in English and French, not Gaelic. In 1366, the English enacted the Statutes of Kilkenny, laws intended to keep English colonists in Ireland from adopting "the manners, fashion, and language of the Irish enemies." Intermarriage was prohibited, as was the use of Gaelic; any English subject heard speaking Gaelic could legally be evicted from his land. The laws even made it illegal for an Englishman to let an Irish traveling musician or storyteller into his home.

The laws did little to stop the English and Irish from mingling in Ireland, however. Throughout the 1400s, England was busy fighting wars abroad, particularly with France, and its attention was diverted from Ireland. By the early 16th century, English influence was mostly confined to the Pale, a strip of land along the east coast centered on Dublin. In 1534, however, England once again grew interested in controlling Ireland. England's King Henry VIII designed a far-reaching policy for Irish conquest.

Henry VIII of England designed a plan for the conquest of Ireland and introduced conflict between Catholics and Protestants.

Oppression and Independence

Despite their differences, the English and Irish shared a common religion: Roman Catholicism. For centuries, Catholicism had been the dominant religion in Europe. But in the 16th century, a new religious movement called the Reformation swept Europe. Touched off by Martin Luther, a German monk and scholar, the Reformation called for rebellion against the Roman Catholic Church. All over the continent, Catholics began questioning church doctrine and practices. Eventually, many gave up Catholicism and established the various churches of what came to be known as the Protestant religion.

Protestantism quickly took hold in many European countries. In England, King Henry VIII made Protestantism the state religion after the Pope refused to grant him a divorce from his wife so that he could marry his mistress, Anne Boleyn. In 1534, he declared himself head of the new Church of England and made Protestantism England's official religion.

England became Protestant, but Ireland, which was insulated from the Reformation and its effects, remained staunchly Catholic. As a result, the conflict that already raged between Ireland and England took on a religious dimension.

Henry VIII himself sparked the first wave of bloodshed between Catholics and Protestants in Ireland. Fearing the threat of Catholic powers outside England, between 1534 and 1537 Henry crushed a rebellion in Ireland and tried to impose the Church of England on the Irish people. He also began a new program to deprive the Catholic Irish of their property and their freedom.

Henry seized Irish tribal lands and pitted clan chiefs against one another in a struggle for his favor. He also encouraged the Catholic chiefs to rebel against Roman authority, offering them "Catholicism without the Pope." He suppressed the monasteries, the heart of Irish Catholicism, and made fugitives of the monks, friars, and priests who would not submit to his supremacy as head of the new church.

Despite English oppression, most Irish Catholics clung to their own religion. But they found it increasingly difficult to hold on to their way of life. When Henry VIII's daughter, Mary I, became queen of England in 1553, she started a colonization program known as "plantation." Under this program, Irish clans were evicted from their lands, and English colonists or Irish people who were loyal to England were "planted" on the land in their place. Clans were scattered and forced to leave their ancestral homes. The traditional Irish society started by the Celts almost 2,000 years earlier was torn apart. Irish people who chose to remain on their land had to serve the new settlers as slaves.

Mary's sister, Elizabeth I, became queen of England in 1558. Called by her loving English subjects, "Good Queen Bess," Elizabeth I was hated by the Irish. She increased the persecution of Catholics by ordering the execution of Irish Catholic priests and bishops and by forbidding Catholic religious services. But courageous Catholics kept their religion alive in secret, and Elizabeth's attempts at repression only awakened a new feeling of unity among the Irish people.

As part of her anti-Catholic campaign, Elizabeth I stepped up the plantation program. In 1571, in retaliation for a failed Catholic uprising in Munster, she seized 400,000 acres (160,000 hectares) of Catholic-owned land in southwest Ireland and turned it over to English settlers. Her forces also carried out military campaigns against the most stubborn Irish clans,

Elizabeth I, the daughter of Henry VIII, increased the persecution of Catholics in Ireland.

notably the O'Neills in the northern part of the island, the O'Byrnes in the east, and the Burkes in the west.

The Irish fought valiantly against the English. An Irish victory against a much larger English force in 1593 inspired more Irish uprisings in Munster, Leinster, and other areas of the island. But the most successful opposition to English rule came from the chieftains of Ulster, in the northeastern section of the island. From the mid-1590's to about 1602, led by Hugh O'Neill, Earl of Tyrone, and Hugh Roe O'Donnell, Earl of Tyrconnel, northern Irish forces fought with Elizabeth's armies.

But despite some triumphs, the struggle ended in defeat. The English laid waste to the Irish countryside and forced the Irish chieftains to bow to English authority. The end of organized Irish resistance in the north came in 1607, when Hugh O'Neill, the last titled descendant of the Celtic king Niall of the Nine Hostages, and 98 other northern Irish Catholic noblemen left Ireland for foreign exile.

This "Flight of the Earls," as it became known, opened the way for English colonization of the north. Between 1603 and 1625, England cleared most of the remaining Irish out of the north and established Ulster Plantation, a settlement of Scottish and English Protestants. Unlike the English settlers in many other parts of Ireland, these northern Protestants remained fiercely loyal to England.

Although they had been defeated, not all northern Irish accepted servitude or exile. Many, especially the former soldiers, hid in the mountains and forests, waiting for the day when they would again rise up against their oppressors.

In 1641, another Catholic-Protestant war broke out; it continued for more than a decade. Thousands of northern Protestant colonists were killed, and many others were driven off the island. For a time, the Ulster Plantation was in danger of collapse.

But in the fall of 1649, Oliver Cromwell, the leader of England's short-lived Republican government, landed at Dublin with an army of 20,000 men. Cromwell was determined to crush the Irish rebellion for good. His first target was the east coast town of Drogheda. After defeating the soldiers who were defending the town, Cromwell's forces massacred almost the entire civilian population—some 3,500 men, women, and children. Within three years after Cromwell's landing, the English forces had captured most of Ireland's major towns and had once again subdued the rebels.

After the surrender of the Irish stronghold of Galway in 1652, the English allowed the remaining Irish soldiers, more than 30,000 men, to leave Ireland for exile in France and Spain. The English then sent many thousands of Irish peasants to England's colonies in the West Indies and Virginia to work as slaves. It is estimated that because of war and deportation, the population of Ireland fell from almost 1.5 million to just over 600,000 between 1641 and 1652.

In 1652, Cromwell enacted the Act of Settlement for Ireland. The act pardoned the poorest peasants but severely punished landowners who had opposed English rule, confiscating their land and granting it to Cromwell's soldiers and others who had supported the English cause. The former landowners were banished to the rocky and desolate province of Connaught, west of the River Shannon. The expression "to Hell or Connaught" was often uttered in despair by those with no other place to go.

English domination of Ireland continued after Cromwell's government fell and the monarchy was restored. By the latter part of the 17th century, England completely controlled Ireland. English landlords owned more than 80 percent of the land, and most of the Irish were reduced to extreme poverty.

In 1685, however, a Catholic king took the British throne. James II (also known as James Stuart) brought new hope to the downtrodden Irish by ending the most severe forms of persecution against Catholics. But the leaders of the Church of England and the Parliament objected to James's pro-Catholic policies, and they invited William of Orange, a Dutch Protestant who was also James's son-in-law, to become king of England.

Seeking to regain his crown, James went to France and then to Ireland, assembling a sizable army of French and Irish Catholics. William, with a force of more than 36,000 English and Dutch Protestants, also went to Ireland, where he was joined by troops from Protestant Ulster. In 1690, the two forces clashed on the banks of the River Boyne.

The Battle of the Boyne ended in a decisive defeat for the Catholics. James fled to France. His army continued to fight as it retreated westward; in 1691, it fought valiantly in a great battle at Aughrim and later in a siege at Limerick. Eventually, however, James's forces were beaten, ending forever the hope of a peaceful Catholic Ireland. In the 1700s, with all of its leaders dead or exiled, Ireland plunged into a long period of almost complete submission to England.

To punish the Catholics for opposing King William, England enacted a set of policies known as the Penal Laws. These laws forbade Catholics to buy land, vote, hold public office, own a gun, or own a horse worth more than five pounds (a price at which only a very poor horse could be bought).

James II ended the persecution of Catholics, but he lost his throne to William of Orange at the Battle of the Boyne.

Catholics were barred from becoming lawyers or teachers, and Catholic schools were outlawed. In addition, religious worship was severely restricted; only the few Catholic priests who had given up all loyalty to James and the Stuarts were allowed to hold services.

English statesman Edmund Burke described the Penal Laws as "a machine . . . as well fitted for the oppression, impoverishment, and degradation of a people, and the debasement in them of human nature itself, as ever proceeded from the perverted ingenuity of man." But as cruel and inhumane as they were, the Penal Laws could not crush the Irish Catholic spirit. Many Catholics held classes in outdoor "hedge schools" and met in secret to keep their faith alive through the dark days.

Toward a United Ireland

With Irish Catholics blocked from every opportunity for advancement, the so-called "Protestant ascendancy" became the dominant class in Ireland. Also known as the Anglo (or English) -Irish ascendancy, this group of newly rich Protestant landowners built magnificent castles in the country and mansions in Dublin.

While these new aristocrats lived lives of luxury, poor Catholic farmers lived near starvation on a diet that consisted almost entirely of potatoes. By 1760, when George III became king of England, criticism of England had begun to grow. Around this time, a street song became the unofficial national anthem of Catholic Ireland:

> Oh, Paddy dear, and did ye hear the news
> > that's goin' round?
> The shamrock is by law forbid to grow
> > on Irish ground.
> No more Saint Patrick's day we'll keep,
> > his color can't be seen,
> For there's a cruel law ag'in the Wearin'
> > o' the Green.

Frustrated in their attempts to gain reforms through lawful means, many Irish Catholics organized secret armed gangs. These gangs, with names such as the White Boys and the Cork Boys, roamed the countryside at night, bent on revenge. They lynched English land agents and tax collectors and attacked Anglo-Irish estates, killing sheep and cattle and destroying fences and buildings. As the oppression of Catholics continued, many Irish Protestants began to sympathize with the Catholics. Slowly, a bond of unity began to grow between all Irish people—Catholics and Protestants—against England.

News of the American Revolution in 1776 and the French Revolution in 1789 made some Irish eager to rebel against their English overlords. In 1791, a young Protestant lawyer named Theobald Wolfe Tone formed the Society of United Irishmen to "abolish all unnatural religious distinctions, [and] to unite all Irishmen against the unjust influence of Great Britain." Soon, the Society had more than 150,000 members.

That same year, England went to war with France. Tone, by now in exile, persuaded the French to back him in an armed rebellion. In December 1796, he sailed with a force of 15,000 French soldiers for Bantry Bay in southwest Ireland.

Bad weather forced Tone's ships to return to France, but the setback was only temporary. By the spring of 1798, rebellion was in the air throughout Ireland. The United Irishmen rose up in several areas—notably Wexford and Arklow—but were promptly defeated by the well-armed and well-trained British soldiers. Tone again attempted to land with a French force; this time, he was captured. He requested a soldier's death before a firing squad, but was instead sentenced to be hanged as a common criminal. Rather than suffer this indignity, he committed suicide in a British prison cell.

In 1803, Robert Emmet followed Tone as the leader of the Society of United Irishmen. A dreamy idealist unsuited to the hard realities of armed

During the Irish Rebellion of 1798, the Irish (on the right) were defeated at Vinegar Hill.

rebellion, Emmet came to symbolize the Irish people's valiant struggle for independence against overwhelming odds. The rebellion he planned ended in a disastrous defeat and his own death by hanging, but the words he spoke at his trial burned into the hearts of people everywhere who yearned for freedom.

"My Lords," he began, "as to why judgment of death and execution should not be passed on me according to law, I have nothing to say." He went on to predict that the Irish would revolt time and time again until they were finally independent of England. He closed his speech with these words: "My ministry is now ended. I am going to my cold and silent grave—my lamp of life is nearly extinguished. I have parted with everything

William Pitt, prime minister under George III, was the architect of the Bill of Union, which made Ireland a part of England.

that was dear to me in this life for my country's cause. . . . Let no man write my epitaph! When my country takes its place among the nations of the earth, then, and not till then, let my epitaph be written. I have done."

Robert Emmet's deeds and words served as a great inspiration to later Irish patriots. Songs and poems were written about the "Darlin' of Erin," as he came to be called, and his portrait hung in a place of honor in thousands of Irish homes. Even today, Irish schoolchildren memorize his last words as a reminder of their ancestors' brave struggle for independence.

Although the rebellions led by Tone and Emmet ended in disaster, they forced England to make some changes in its treatment of the Irish. Even before the uprising of 1798, the English prime minister William Pitt had decided that the only way to keep control of the Irish was to transfer all of Ireland's political power to the English Parliament and merge Ireland's economy with England's. The Act of Union of 1800 did this by making Ireland an official part of Great Britain. Although many Irish, even the members of the Anglo-Irish ascendancy, were against this act, Pitt bribed enough members of Ireland's Parliament to ensure its passage.

To help gain support for the Act, Pitt had promised the Irish that he would work for repeal of the hated Penal Laws that still made most Irish Catholics second-class citizens. But King George III refused Pitt's request for repeal. As a result, the Penal Laws remained in effect until 1829, when Daniel O'Connell won his long fight for Irish political freedom. Known as the "Liberator of Ireland," O'Connell was a brilliant orator whose fiery speeches inspired the Irish peasants to seek freedom. His powerful voice could rise over the noise of the largest crowds. In 1823, O'Connell formed the Catholic Society to push for increased rights for Irish Catholics. Then, in 1828, he was elected to the English Parliament as the representative of County Clare.

O'Connell was forbidden to take his seat in Parliament because the Penal Laws stated that Catholics could not hold elected office. The British government knew that O'Connell had the support of millions of Irish Catholics, and it wanted to prevent another uprising. It passed the Catholic Emancipation Act in 1829. This act granted Irish Catholics many of the rights denied them by the Penal Laws, including the right to hold elected office.

The Emancipation Act was a great political victory—but for the majority of Irish Catholics, it had little meaning. Living in extreme poverty and struggling just to stay alive, they had little interest in politics. In 1835, French writer Alexis de Tocqueville visited Ireland and described the pathetic life of the Catholic peasants this way: "Mud walls; thatched roofs; one room; no chimney; smoke comes out of the door . . . the population looks very wretched. Most of them are dressed in clothes with holes or very much patched. Most of them are barefoot and bareheaded."

These conditions led O'Connell, supported by a new group of patriots known as the Young Ireland movement, to continue his fight for Irish rights. In 1841, he planned a peaceful rally to demonstrate against the Act of Union. The rally was to be held on the battlefield of Clontarf, where Brian Boru had defeated the Vikings in 1014; thousands of people were expected to attend. But the British government ordered the rally canceled

Living conditions in rural Ireland have been dismal and primitive throughout its history.

and threatened to use force to break it up if it was held. Worried about possible bloodshed, O'Connell called off the demonstration. His disappointed followers turned away from him and, broken in spirit, he died a few years later.

O'Connell's failure to win repeal of the Act of Union was followed in 1845 by the worst disaster ever to hit Ireland—the potato famine. Over a period of three years, most of Ireland's potato crop—the main source of food for millions of peasants—was destroyed by disease. Mass starvation resulted. More than 1.5 million people died, and another 1 million were forced to leave Ireland for the United States and other lands.

The British government did little to help the Irish during the famine. Despite the starvation of millions, the British continued to export Irish food crops and cattle to England. Other nations tried to send aid, but the hunger was too widespread. By 1851, Ireland's population had shrunk from 8 million to about 6 million.

Even after the famine ended, the rural areas remained poor and the population continued to fall. Talk of armed rebellion increased. In 1858, Irish rebels in England and Ireland formed the Irish Republican Brotherhood, and Irish immigrants in the United States started a secret society called the Fenian Brotherhood (after the Fianna Celtic hero Finn Mac-Cool's legendary band of warriors).

Both groups called for Ireland's complete independence from England. The Fenians turned to violence to accomplish their goals. They set off bombs in British sectors and led several armed uprisings. But by 1867, these movements, like all the others, had been crushed by England, ending armed rebellion for the next 50 years.

Home Rule

Although the Fenians' armed rebellions had been quashed, others continued the movement for Irish independence through peaceful means. In the 1870s and 1880s, a plan called home rule became an important issue. This plan called for Ireland to govern its own domestic matters while England continued to control its international affairs.

The most important champion of home rule was Charles Stewart Parnell. Although Parnell was a Protestant landowner, he earned the support of Catholics for his impassioned defense of the rights of tenant farmers against exploitation by landlords. He became the leader of the Irish group in the English Parliament, where he was able to achieve many reforms.

In the struggle for home rule, Parnell enlisted the support of William Gladstone, England's prime minister. But despite Gladstone's influence, Parliament defeated home rule bills in 1886 and again in 1892. The main opposition to home rule came from the wealthy Protestants in the northern part of Ireland, who feared that home rule would lead to Catholic domination.

Despite the defeat of home rule, the Irish people's spirit of independence continued to grow. In 1893, Douglas Hyde and Eoin MacNeill founded the Gaelic League to revive Ireland's ancient Gaelic traditions. The league worked to make Gaelic legends, songs, dances, and crafts known to the Irish people. It also brought back the use of the Gaelic language. As a result, the Irish people developed a new pride in their heritage and a new determination to separate themselves from England.

In this same spirit, a Dublin newspaperman named Arthur Griffith founded a society known as Sinn Fein (pronounced shin fane) in 1905. Sinn Fein (Gaelic for "ourselves alone") encouraged the Irish people to refuse to pay English taxes and to renew their struggle for cultural and political independence.

Sinn Fein's influence grew throughout the early 1900s, leading to the revival of the Irish Republican Brotherhood and the idea of another armed rebellion. The Brotherhood was led by Padraic Henry Pearse, a poet and schoolteacher. In 1915, at the funeral of martyred Irish patriot Jeremiah O'Donovan Rossa, Pearse demonstrated his love of country and his fiery oratorical skills: "We pledge to Ireland our love, and we pledge to English rule in Ireland our hate. . . . The Defenders of this Realm . . . think that they have pacified Ireland . . . the fools, the fools, the fools! They have left us our Fenian dead, and while Ireland holds these graves Ireland unfree will never be at peace."

In early 1916, Pearse—along with other leaders—planned an armed uprising known as the Easter Rebellion. On Easter Monday, April 24, 1916, Pearse led his followers, numbering around 1,200 men, into central Dublin. Because of several mix-ups, his force was less than half of what he had expected; furthermore, a hoped-for shipment of arms had been inter-cepted by the British. But though they were heavily outnumbered, the rebels captured several buildings.

Pearse himself led one group of rebels into the Dublin post office, which he declared the headquarters of the new provisional Irish Republi-can government. After raising the orange, white, and green rebel flag, Pearse mounted the front steps and read his now-famous proclamation that begins, "Irishmen and Irishwomen: In the name of God and the dead generations from which she receives her old tradition of nationhood, Ire-land, through us, summons her children to her flag and strikes for her freedom."

(continued on page 73)

SCENES OF
IRELAND

▲ *A Connemara pony and foal are groomed by a young woman in Galway.*

◄ *Hore Abbey, a Cistercian monastery established in 1272, seen from the Rock of Cashel.*

◄ *Eighteenth-century Irish architecture is illustrated by this splendid doorway in Dublin.*

◄ The Round Tower of
Glendalough Abbey was
built by priests in the
Middle Ages as a defense
against Viking raids.

∨ This family glows with Celtic vigor and grace.

▲ *Christ the King Cathedral in Galway was completed in 1965.*

➤ An 18th-century shop in Dublin conjures up the city's elegant past.

◄ Dingle Bay on the west coast provides an excellent harbor for fishing and merchant vessels.

< 70 >

∧ *The beauty and serenity of much of the Irish countryside are at odds with the turbulence of the country's history.*

AR OSCAILT DE DOMHNAIGH 2–5ᴾᴹ   LAETHE NA SEACHTAINE 10ᴀᴍ–6ᴾᴹ
AR OSCAILT GO DÉANACH DÉARDAOIN GO 9ᴾᴹ

≺ *Two Irish policemen are posted in front of a Gaelic street sign.*

This cross in Glendalough ➤
Abbey is a typical example
of a unique Celtic design.

▲ *Dublin's St. Patrick's Day parade is traditionally an occasion of much pomp and splendor.*

▼ *The rural Irish landscape is dotted with thatched cottages built to an ancient design.*

While Pearse and his followers held the post office, the British were busy amassing an army of 12,000 soldiers. Soon, fighting broke out; during the week-long battle that followed, the streets of Dublin were filled with gunfire and explosions. A British gunboat on the River Liffey demolished many buildings and set the post office ablaze. When the fighting was over, 50 rebels, 216 civilians, and 130 British soldiers lay dead.

The surviving rebel leaders, including Pearse, were executed before a firing squad. One leader, James Connolly, had been so badly wounded in the fighting that he faced the firing squad strapped to a chair. Other rebels were imprisoned in England.

Independence

Instead of discouraging rebellion, as the British government intended, the executions of Padraic Pearse and the other rebel leaders outraged the Irish people and led to their final fight for freedom. In the general election of 1918, the Irish voted 73 Sinn Fein candidates into the British Parliament. But the members refused to take their seats; instead, they set up their own assembly called Dail Eireann (Irish House of Deputies). They declared the Dail Eireann as the Irish Parliament, and elected Eamon De Valera, the most prominent survivor of the Easter Rebellion, as its first president. De Valera discouraged further violence, preaching what he called "passive resistance" instead.

The British government not only refused to recognize the new Irish government, it jailed De Valera and other leaders. It fell to the Irish Republican Army (IRA), as the rebels now called themselves, to carry on the struggle.

The IRA was led by Michael Collins, known as the "Big Fellow." A brash, ruthless commander who used terrorism to achieve his goals, Collins led the IRA in a hit-and-run war that came to be known as the Troubles. Avoiding big battles like the Easter Rebellion, they concentrated instead on conducting surprise raids on British garrisons or patrols. For example, on November 21, 1920, a squad of IRA gunmen killed 14 British

During the Easter Rebellion of 1916, automobiles were used to build barricades.

secret agents sent to infiltrate the IRA. Most of the victims were shot in their beds or as they answered a knock at the door. This day is now known in Ireland as Bloody Sunday.

The 15,000-member IRA was greatly outnumbered by the British, who had more than 70,000 troops and an auxiliary police unit known as the Black and Tans. Nevertheless, bitter fighting continued for more than two years. Meanwhile, De Valera escaped from prison in England and returned to assume the presidency of the Dail Eireann.

The British government eventually realized that the Irish people were determined to win their freedom at all costs. In 1920, the British proposed a compromise treaty called the Government of Ireland Act. Under the terms of this act, Ireland was to be divided into two separate sections—one made up of the six primarily Protestant northeastern counties (most of the province of Ulster), and one made up of the remaining 26 counties, which were predominantly Catholic. Ulster was to be renamed Northern Ireland and made an official member of the United Kingdom (which already included England, Scotland, and Wales). The rest of the island was to become the Irish Free State—an independent dominion, much like Canada, that retained ties to the United Kingdom.

The leaders in the north agreed to this British proposal for dividing Ireland, but De Valera and the IRA rejected it, and more fighting ensued. Finally, in late 1921, moderate elements of the Sinn Fein overruled De Valera and approved the Government of Ireland Act. It was ratified (made into law) on January 14, 1922.

As soon as the Act was ratified, a bitter civil war broke out between De Valera's Republicans, who wanted a totally independent Ireland, and the Free State government (one of whose leaders was former IRA chief Michael Collins), which favored the agreement with England. Although the Irish Civil War ended in defeat for the Republicans, De Valera again was elected to the Dail, where he continued to work for Irish independence.

In 1926, De Valera split with Sinn Fein and formed a new political party, Fianna Fail ("warriors of destiny"). Throughout the 1920s, Fianna Fail steadily grew in power. In 1932, it gained control of the Irish Free State government and elected De Valera president of the Free State's executive committee. In this capacity, and later as the Free State's prime minister (from 1937 to 1948), he loosened many of Ireland's ties with England.

A new constitution in 1937 gave Ireland even more independence, establishing it as a sovereign nation within the British Commonwealth. Finally, in late 1948, the Irish Free State prime minister John A. Costello introduced a bill to the Dail that would "end, and end forever, in a simple unequivocal way, the country's long and tragic association with the British Crown." Support for the bill was unanimous. On April 18, 1949, the Dail declared the 26 southern counties to be the totally independent Republic of Ireland—free from England at last.

Leinster House, now the meeting place of the Dail Eirann, was built by the German architect Cassels in 1745 for the first Duke of Leinster.

Government and Economy

Ireland's constitution reflects a deeply rooted love of independence and a strong respect for human rights. Adopted by the Irish Free State in 1937, this document became the constitution of the Republic of Ireland in 1949. It sets forth the basic principles for which Ireland stands. It affirms the country's "devotion to the ideal of peace and friendly cooperation amongst nations founded on international peace and morality" and guarantees all the republic's citizens certain basic rights, including the right to "be held equal before the law." It also designates Ireland's form of government and guarantees all adult citizens the right to choose government leaders in free elections.

The Republic of Ireland has a form of government known as a parliamentary democracy. It consists of a president, a prime minister, and a two-chambered Parliament, called in Gaelic the *Oireachtas*. The president, elected by direct vote for a seven-year term, may serve no more than two terms. As Ireland's representative in international affairs, the president officially appoints the prime minister and other government officials, signs or vetoes laws, and commands the republic's armed forces.

Although the president is the official head of state, the prime minister actually runs the government on a daily basis. He oversees the Parliament and appoints some of its members to run various government departments. The prime minister, nominated by the lower house of Parliament and appointed by the president, serves for a maximum of five years.

Ireland's Parliament consists of two lawmaking houses, the Dail Eireann (Irish House of Deputies) and the Seanad Eireann (Irish Senate). The lower house, the Dail, has 166 members, all of whom are elected by the public to serve five-year terms. The Dail's major duties are to make laws and nominate the prime minister.

The Seanad, or upper house, has 60 members, some elected by the Dail and some appointed by the prime minister. Its members have no fixed terms, but a new Seanad must be selected within 90 days of the general elections for the Dail. The Seanad is responsible for approving laws passed to it from the Dial. It can reject or change any laws submitted to it, with the exception of funding bills, which it cannot change. The Seanad can also create its own bills.

Local government is based on Ireland's counties and county boroughs. The republic is divided into 27 administrative counties, each of

Ireland's legal system, centered in this Dublin building, consists of local circuit and district courts, a High Court, and the Supreme Court.

which is governed by a county council. (Although Ireland has only 26 counties, County Tipperary is divided into two administrative districts.) The other local divisions are: 4 county boroughs (Dublin, Cork, Limerick, and Waterford), each of which is governed by a borough council; 7 municipal boroughs, each governed by a municipal corporation; 49 urban (city) districts, headed by urban district councils; and 28 towns, led by town commissioners.

The people elect these local authorities about every five years. The main duties of local government are to administer local affairs and to collect local taxes that help pay for roads, schools, public health and sanitation services, and police and firefighting.

Ireland has four major political parties: the Fianna Fail ("warriors of destiny"), the Fine Gael ("the Gaelic people"), the Labour party, and the Progressive Democrats. These parties hold most of the seats in the Dail; there also are a number of smaller parties and independent candidates.

The party that wins the majority of seats in the general elections becomes the ruling party, and its leader is usually elected prime minister. Sometimes, if the election results are close, two parties will form a coalition government. For example, in 1982 the Fianna Fail won 75 seats, the Fine Gael won 70, and the Labour party won 16. In order to prevent the Fianna Fail from becoming the ruling party, the Fine Gael and the Labour party banded together to form a Fine Gael-Labour coalition government. They then elected Fine Gael leader Garret FitzGerald to the prime minister's seat.

In the general elections held in 1985, Fine Gael lost to the Fianna Fail. The leader of the Fianna Fail, Charles Haughey, was narrowly elected prime minister by the Parliament. Unless he loses the confidence of the Parliament, Haughey will head the government until the general election in 1990.

Ireland's legal system consists of local circuit and district courts, a High Court (which hears major criminal cases and appeals), and the Supreme Court, the highest court in the land. There are also special crimi-

This is one of 28 electrical plants that provide power for industry. It is fired by "brown gold"—peat from the bogs.

nal courts, set up to control terrorism. In the circuit and district courts and the High Court, the right to trial by jury is guaranteed in both civil and criminal cases. But in the special criminal courts, a panel of judges makes rulings without the aid of a jury.

Law enforcement is the responsibility of the Department of Justice, led by a commissioner. The commissioner supervises the 10,000-member Garda Siochana (civil guard), the nation's unarmed police force. Irish police officers do not carry guns except in special circumstances.

Economy

Ireland has a fairly diverse economy. Slightly more than 32 percent of the work force is employed in industry, including manufacturing, mining, and energy production. About 19 percent works in agriculture, forestry, and fishing. The remaining 49 percent of Ireland's labor force works in service-related occupations in government, education, health care, transportation, sales, and other areas.

Since the early 1970s, the Irish economy has undergone a steady transformation. Once it was based on agriculture, but now it is based on industry. This economic change, known as industrialization, has given the Irish people many benefits, including a better standard of living and improved education. But it has produced problems as well. Like many newly industrialized countries, Ireland has experienced some serious growing pains.

Throughout the 1970s, the Irish government pursued a policy of rapid industrialization and economic growth. One of its first steps toward this goal was to join the European Economic Community (EEC) in 1973. The EEC, also known as the Common Market, is an organization of European countries—including Great Britain, France, West Germany, and many others—that cooperate for mutual economic benefit. As a member of the EEC, Ireland can sell its products to other member countries without paying customs duties. This lets Irish companies sell their goods at lower prices, and this increases sales.

After joining the EEC, Ireland began to encourage foreign companies to invest in Ireland. The government offered companies tax holidays (periods of no taxation) and other incentives. Many foreign companies came to the island; at one point more than 400 U.S. companies had factories in Ireland. Companies from Great Britain, West Germany, the Netherlands, Japan, Canada, and many other countries also built factories.

The new factories provided much-needed jobs for the Irish people and a new prosperity for the republic. By 1981, foreign investment in Irish factories totaled U.S. $4 billion, and foreign companies employed almost one-third of Ireland's labor force. Ireland's industrial sector was one of the fastest growing in Western Europe.

But in the early 1980s, foreign investment began to decline, and factories began laying off workers. The national debt—the amount of money owed by the government—doubled in just four years. By 1987, Ireland was facing its worst economic crisis in more than half a century. Individual income taxes averaged about 40 percent, the highest in Western Europe.

Glittering Waterford crystal is one of Ireland's most celebrated products. It is sold in many countries around the world, earning foreign exchange income for Ireland.

About 18 percent of the work force was unemployed, and the number of welfare recipients had tripled since 1980. Unable to find work at home, tens of thousands of young people began leaving Ireland for the United States, Australia, and other countries.

Many industries remain, although massive amounts of foreign investment have been withdrawn. Ireland's factories, located mainly in Dublin and other large cities, produce a variety of goods for export as well as for sale at home. Major products include cloth, paper, metals, and furniture. The traditional industries of beer brewing, whiskey distilling, and food processing continue to be important, and a growing electronics industry produces computers and related equipment. Other important industries include glassware, printing, chemicals, and cement and other construction materials. But the Republic still imports more goods than it exports, and its economic problems demand attention. The government believes that continued industrialization will provide more jobs.

Agriculture

For centuries, most of Ireland's people were farmers, and agriculture was the country's most important economic activity. But today most of the Irish work in towns and cities. Over the past decade and a half, the number of farms in Ireland has steadily decreased. Small family farms, once the backbone of Irish agriculture, are rapidly disappearing from the countryside; as the older farmers die, their heirs—no longer interested in farming—sell the land.

Despite the decrease in the number of farms and farmers, Irish agriculture still has significant economic importance. More than two-thirds of Ireland's area remains farmland, and 19 percent of the labor force works in agriculture. Larger farms, some run by corporations, are using modern agricultural methods and equipment to increase efficiency and productivity.

Livestock is the primary agricultural product. Almost every farm keeps some cattle. The island's mild climate and fertile soils are ideal for cattle raising, and about 90 percent of all farmland is pasture. Young cattle are reared mainly in the milk-producing counties in Ireland's south and west, and then fattened in the lush pastures of the central plain.

Ireland has numerous dairy farms. Larger dairies use expensive, mechanized milking equipment, but most small family farmers still milk their cows by hand. Large and small farmers alike sell their milk to local dairy cooperatives that make and market butter, cheese, and milk powder. Ireland's beef cattle and dairy products are its top agricultural exports and are recognized as among the finest in the world. Irish farmers also raise pigs, sheep, and horses.

Only about 10 percent of Ireland's farmland is used for growing crops. Potatoes, barley, wheat, and sugar beets are among the most widely grown crops.

Other Economic Activities

Besides manufacturing and farming, many other industries contribute to Ireland's economy. The sea around Ireland teems with many types of fish and shellfish, and commercial fishing is slowly growing in economic importance. For centuries, Ireland did not have a noteworthy fishing industry, but today an increasingly modern fishing fleet hauls in large catches of herring, mackerel, lobster, salmon, and other varieties for sale at home and abroad.

Irish arts and crafts are valued the world over for beauty and fine workmanship. Hand-knit wool sweaters, musical instruments, crystal, and pottery are exported and also sold to tourists. In recent years, Irish artisans have started forming cooperatives to help them market their goods more effectively. But these artisans do more than just contribute to the

Ireland has numerous dairy farms. Larger dairies use expensive mechanized milking equipment, but most small farmers still milk by hand.

economy. By keeping the old crafts alive, they also help to preserve Ireland's rich cultural heritage.

Tourism has become very important to the Irish economy. Every year, millions of people from all over the world visit Ireland; in fact, almost as many people visit each year as actually live on the island. Tourists spend money in hotels, restaurants, shops, and other attractions, creating jobs for thousands of Irish workers and pumping much-needed foreign currency into the Irish economy.

The thatched and whitewashed cottages in Curracloe are typical of Ireland's rural architecture.

Life and Customs

For centuries, the Irish countryside has been famous for its simple beauty. In the early 20th century, the Irish poet and dramatist John Millington Synge wrote about a home in the Aran Islands:

> The kitchen itself, where I spend most of my time, is full of beauty and distinction. The red dresses of the women who cluster around the fire on their stools give a glow of almost Eastern richness, and the walls have been toned by the turf smoke to a soft brown that blends with the grey earth color of the floor. Many sorts of fishing tackle, and the nets and oilskins of the men, are hung upon the walls or among the open rafters. . . . Every article . . . has an almost personal character, which gives this simple life, where all art is unknown, something of the artistic beauty of medieval life.

Today, the traditional Ireland of thatch-roofed cottages and red-skirted colleens (girls) has largely disappeared. Dublin, Cork, and the other cities bustle with a distinctly modern hum. The larger Irish towns look much like those in any other industrialized nation, with modern homes, shopping centers, factories, and office buildings. In the rural areas, new farmhouses have replaced many of the old stone cottages, and most farms now have electricity, telephones, and other modern conveniences.

In some parts of Ireland, however, the old way of life endures. The farming areas of the west and southwest and the islands recall an earlier time. This is especially true of the tiny Aran Islands; they have changed little since Synge described them at the turn of the century.

The Aran Islands

Three small islands located at the entrance to Galway Bay make up the Arans. The largest, Inishmore (also called Big Island), is 11 miles (18 kilometers) long; the other two, Inishmaan and Inisheer, are scarcely one-quarter this size. Together, the islands total only 18 square miles (47 square kilometers) and have fewer than 2,000 inhabitants. Here, the people live much as they have for centuries. Their stone-walled, thatch-roofed cottages usually are heated only by a fireplace. Few have telephones, and many are without electricity or indoor plumbing.

The islands consist mainly of rock, so only about a third of the land is under cultivation. The thin soil, constantly eroded by heavy wind and rain, must be frequently renewed. The people do this by carrying seaweed and sand from the beach and mixing it with bits of clay. They slowly pile this mixture up, layer by layer, until it is deep enough to plant potatoes. Virtually all of the usable soil on the islands has been created by generations of islanders following this process.

High stone walls, built of rocks cleared from the land, separate the farms, shelter the tiny fields from wind, and form pens for horses, cattle, and sheep. These walls have no gates; to let an animal out of a field, part of the wall must be removed. Every wall has a small section of loosely piled stones for this purpose.

The islands have no trees or peat bogs, so fuel for heating and cooking must be brought by boat from the mainland. At one time, sailing craft known as hookers brought loads of peat from Connemara on the mainland. A loaded hooker would sail back and forth offshore as the islanders called out their bids for its cargo. When the hooker's captain was satisfied with the price, he would dock and sell the peat to the highest bidder. Today, the hookers have been replaced by motorized vessels, which bring

The Aran Islands consist mainly of rock, so only about one third of the land can be cultivated.

peat on a regular schedule. But peat has become increasingly expensive, and many Aran islanders now heat their homes with bottled gas or coal imported from England.

Although Inishmore has a small airstrip, a single steamship provides the main connection between the islands and the mainland. The ship ferries passengers, livestock, mail, and supplies between the islands and Galway, a mainland town some 30 miles (48 km) away. It can dock only at Inishmore's harbor of Kilronan; on the other islands, the rocky coast prevents landing.

People on Inishmaan and Inisheer must row out to meet the steamer in small boats called *curraghs*. For generations, islanders have depended on these craft for transportation. Made of tarred canvas stretched tightly over a wooden frame, they are propelled by long, narrow-bladed oars. When handled skillfully, a curragh skims lightly over the rough seas.

A curragh does not require a dock to land. It can easily be beached on any of the sandy pockets that dot the rocky shore. The crew simply jumps out into the surf before the curragh's bow touches the sand, then picks up the lightweight craft and carries it out of the reach of the waves. Today, a few islanders have modern boats made of fiberglass or aluminum, but most still use the traditional curraghs.

Family Life

Although most Irish homes have modern conveniences, Irish families still cling to many of the traditional ways of life. One of the most important traditions is an extremely strong love of family. Families are considered so important that the Irish Constitution includes a passage recognizing "the family as the natural primary and fundamental unit group of Society, and as a moral institution possessing inalienable . . . rights. . . ." Furthermore, it states that the government "guarantees to protect the Family . . . as indispensable to the welfare of the Nation."

The Irish take care of all family members. Very rarely is an elderly relative put in a nursing home or an orphaned child sent to a foster home or orphanage; families usually welcome any relative who needs a home. It is common for many family members—grandparents, parents, children, aunts, uncles, and cousins—to live together under one roof.

Until recently, many Irish men and women delayed marriage and remained at home with their parents beyond the age of 30. This was due in part to a scarcity of jobs and farmland, but it also was due to the strong bonds between Irish children and their parents. Even today, the average age of marriage in Ireland is well over 25.

Although recent years have brought some changes, many Irish families retain traditional roles. The women do most of the cooking, household chores, and child-rearing, while the men usually bring home the paychecks. Although women recently have begun to enter the work force in greater numbers, wages for women are usually far lower than those for men, and opportunities are limited in many fields.

Religion

Almost 97 percent of the people in the Republic of Ireland are Catholic. For most, to be Irish is to be Catholic; the two are almost inseparable.

The devotion of the Irish to their church can be considered both a blessing and a curse. Throughout Ireland's history, the Irish people have been persecuted because of their religion. The English Penal Laws of the 18th century, for example, stripped Catholics of most of the basic rights that people take for granted today. Irish Catholics were forbidden to practice their religion, to own more than a minimal amount of property, and to vote or hold public office. But the bitter years of religious persecution brought the Irish people close together, forging a unity that eventually enabled them to win their struggle for independence from England.

An Irish family group poses outside their cottage in Galway County. Family life is vitally important in Irish culture.

Today, the Catholic church still plays a vital role in the life of almost every Irish citizen. Although the Irish Constitution guarantees religious freedom to all, it acknowledges "the special position of the Holy Catholic Apostolic and Roman Church as the guardian of faith professed by the great majority of citizens." The dominance of Catholicism leaves little separation between church and state; since virtually every government official is Catholic, the government naturally is deeply influenced by the church. Most of the Irish people see nothing wrong with this—after all, their own lives are also guided by the church.

Just as the Catholic church is the center of almost every Irish town, the local parish priest is just about the most important person in town. He is deeply involved with almost every activity, and the people consult him for advice and guidance not only in spiritual and family matters, but also in business decisions, legal disputes, political arguments, and even the membership of the local sports teams. In many of the smaller towns, the priest is the final authority on numerous aspects of social life.

Education and Health

The Irish people place great emphasis on education. Irish children are required by law to attend school from age 6 to age 15. In primary school, children study reading, writing, mathematics, and other subjects. They also learn about their Irish heritage, including traditional stories, music, and crafts. Virtually all of Ireland's public elementary schools are under the control of the Catholic church.

In second-level education (high school), Irish teenagers can choose from several courses of study. Students may select the general college preparatory curriculum or specialized vocational classes that teach the skills needed for a wide range of professions.

After completing their second-level education, some students choose to go on to a college or university. Ireland has several well-known institutions of higher learning. Trinity College (also known as the University of Dublin) is Ireland's oldest and most famous university, founded in 1591.

Trinity College is Ireland's oldest and most famous university. It was founded in Dublin in 1591.

The National University is the country's largest, with more than 15,000 students in its three branches. There are several fine medical schools. Budding artists may attend the National College of Art and Design in Dublin.

Along with English, all Irish students also learn how to speak and write Gaelic, the ancient language brought to Ireland by the Celts about 2,000 years ago. England outlawed the use of Gaelic (also called Irish) for a time in the 18th and 19th centuries, but the Irish people refused to let it die. During the struggle for independence from England, Irish patriots sparked a revival of all things Gaelic, including language, sports, and customs. In 1893, Douglas Hyde and Eoin MacNeill founded the Gaelic League to restore Ireland's national language, and in 1922 the Irish Free State government made Gaelic a compulsory school subject.

Today, even though Gaelic is the Republic of Ireland's official national language and is taught in schools, only about one-quarter of the Irish people can speak it fluently, and only about 50,000 use it as their primary language. The Gaelic-speaking areas, mainly in the west of the island, are known as the Gaeltacht. By contrast, nearly every Irish person can speak English, which is now Ireland's predominant language.

Overall, the Irish are a very healthy people. The average life expectancy for women is around 75 years, and for men, around 70 years. The minister of health, helped by local health authorities, runs Ireland's national health program. This program entitles all Irish citizens to certain health care services free of charge, including physical examinations for school-age children, child welfare clinics, and treatment for infectious diseases. Charges for other treatments and services are based on the person's ability to pay.

Transportation and Communication

Ireland's road system consists of about 10,000 miles (16,000 km) of highway and more than 45,000 miles (72,000 km) of secondary roads. There are more than a half-million registered vehicles on Ireland's roadways. About 70 percent of these are automobiles—an average of about 12.5 cars for every 100 people.

The country's inland canal system, once an important shipping route, is no longer in use today. Large ships use the major seaports, which include Dublin, Cork, Waterford, Dun Laoghaire, Limerick, Galway, and Drogheda. International airports are located at Dublin, Shannon, and Cork.

Ireland has seven daily newspapers. Five are published in Dublin, two in Cork. Four of these are distributed throughout the country. There are also five national Sunday papers.

The government owns and operates Ireland's radio and television stations and its telephone company. To receive television broadcasts, people must pay an annual fee.

Sports and Pastimes

Sports and games are an integral part of Irish life. Several of the sports played in Ireland date from the time of the ancient Celts. The most popular are hurling and Gaelic football.

Hurling, somewhat similar to lacrosse, is played on a large grass field, known as a pitch, by two teams of 15 players each. The object of the game is to hurl a small leather ball between closely spaced goalposts using a long, broad-ended stick, known as a hurley or *caman*. The action is fast and furious; the Irish call hurling "the world's fastest sport." Considered the "most Irish" of all sports, hurling has legendary origins. The famous epic poem "The Cattle Raid of Cooley" refers to the Celtic hero Cuchulainn's prowess at hurling.

In a hurling match at Ireland's National Games, Kilkenny goes up against Cork in Wembley Stadium.

Although not as ancient as hurling, Gaelic football is equally popular. Despite its name, it has little in common with the American variety of the game; it is actually closer to a combination of soccer and rugby. It is played in two 40-minute periods with no timeouts, and the players wear virtually no protective clothing. Both hurling and Gaelic football are played by amateur teams representing each of Ireland's counties. The seasons of both sports culminate in the All-Ireland matches, held in Dublin's Croke Park before crowds of up to 90,000 fans.

Another uniquely Irish sport is road bowling. Rarely played outside County Cork (and County Armagh in Northern Ireland), road bowling has a simple object: to advance the ball over the finish line in the fewest number of throws. The ball, known as a bullet, is a 28-ounce piece of solid cast iron. The course, laid out over country roads, may be up to several miles long.

In addition to these traditional Celtic games, the Irish compete in many Western sports, including soccer, rugby, cricket, boxing, and track and field. In fact, many Irish long-distance runners are world-renowned. Other popular games include darts, chess, bridge, and bingo.

The Irish have long been fascinated by horses and horse racing. Ireland has more than two dozen racetracks. The most famous races include the Irish Derby, held each June in Kildare, and the Irish Grand National, held near Dublin during Easter week. The number-one social event in all of Ireland is the Dublin Horse Show. Held every summer, it draws riders and horse lovers from all over Europe.

The Arts

Ireland has a long musical heritage in which the Irish take pride. In fact, the national emblem is the harp, an instrument that has been played in Ireland for centuries. Irish folk songs, sung to the accompaniment of the harp and other traditional instruments, such as the fiddle, the flute, and the penny whistle, relate the stories of Irish heroes, great loves won and lost, and the undying love of the Irish people for their homeland. Today,

Irish bands such as the Chieftains and the Bothy Band tour the world spreading traditional Irish music.

The Irish have a great love for all the arts—painting, sculpture, music, and especially literature. The Irish government encourages artists with financial incentives. Writers, composers, painters, and sculptors of any nationality who live in Ireland do not have to pay taxes on their earnings from works judged to have "artistic or cultural merit." Because of this policy, many creative people from around the world now call Ireland their home.

George Bernard Shaw, Ireland's most famous playwright, wrote more than 50 plays.

A Love of Language

The Irish are born storytellers and masters of language. Through the centuries, Irish writers have left an enduring legacy of great literature. Professional storytellers still command a wide audience for their performances of traditional tales. Even the Irish people who do not write or tell stories professionally display a love of language in their everyday conversations. As an admiring Englishman once observed, "However commonplace may be the opinions they express, these opinions are delivered with such a clarity of phrasing and such an astounding air of conviction that the dazzled visitor feels that the Oracle has spoken at last."

This love of words goes back to the dawn of Irish history. The ancient Celts, or Gaels, excelled in storytelling. Their Druid priests created a vast body of legends. Later Celtic poets, known as *file*, trained for years in their art and held high positions in society. For centuries, the file passed down the tales of the heroes and heroines of pre-Christian Ireland.

Not until the 5th century A.D. did the Celts begin writing down Ireland's tales and legends. Encouraged by Catholic missionaries, Celtic monks began the long task of recording the stories in the Gaelic language. In producing these hand-written documents, they created Ireland's first written literature. In fact, Ireland was the first European country north of Italy to produce a body of literature in its native language.

Ireland's ancient tales fall into four categories. The first includes stories of heroes from before the Celts who believed in a magical Land of Youth, where old age and death were unknown. The second, from around the 1st century A.D., includes stories of the legendary hero Cuchulainn's single-handed defense of Ulster, the tragic tales of Dierdre and the Sons of Usna, and the epic poem "The Cattle Raid of Cooley." The third category, dating from around the 3rd century, consists of stories of Cormac Mac Art, Ireland's first high king, his court at the palace of Tara, and his warriors, the Fianna. Famous tales in this category include the love story of Diarmid and Grania and the exploits of the Fianna warrior Finn MacCool. The fourth category consists of around 70 stories about a variety of legendary and historical figures.

From medieval times to the modern era, Irish writers have drawn on these traditional tales for their own work. One tale, the story of Dierdre, has been the basis for many modern works of romance and tragedy. The 20th-century poet and dramatist William Butler Yeats wrote five plays based on the exploits of Cuchulainn.

But the most famous Celtic book does not deal with Celtic legends. Rather, it is an illuminated manuscript of the four Gospels of the New Testament in Latin, with intricate illustrations and decorative borders. Known as the Book of Kells, this great work, which now is on display at the Trinity College Library in Dublin, is believed to have been produced in the late 8th century by the monks of Iona, an island off the west coast of Scotland. When Vikings invaded the area, the monks fled with their precious manuscript to Kells, a monastery located about 35 miles (56 kilometers) northwest of Dublin. Today the Book of Kells is considered Ireland's most valuable Celtic artifact and stands as a symbol of the Irish people's religious devotion.

The beginning of written literature did not end Ireland's oral storytelling tradition. During the period of Norman rule, poet-singers known as bards composed and recited epic poems. After completing a six-year course of study, a bard could look forward to high social status and gifts of money, horses, or land from a rich benefactor in return for a fine piece of verse. During the 18th century, when the English Penal Laws forbade the use of the Gaelic language, storytellers secretly kept the old Irish culture alive. In the remote villages, the storyteller was almost as revered as the priest.

Today, Ireland's oral tradition is alive and well. The ancient tales are recited by professional storytellers as well as by almost every parent or grandparent in Ireland. Every Irish child learns the stories, for example, of Finn MacCool and the Fianna warriors, or of Saint Finnabar, who slew Ireland's last dragon. In this way, the ancient legends continue to fire the Irish imagination.

A tiny nation, Ireland has produced more than its share of great writers. Many of the world's leading literary figures before 1900 were Irish or had an Irish background. One of these was the satirist Jonathan Swift (1667–1745), dean of Saint Patrick's Cathedral in Dublin. His satires (works that ridicule human vice and folly) include "A Modest Proposal," *A Tale of a Tub*, and *Gulliver's Travels*. Other notable pre-20th-century writers with Irish backgrounds include William Congreve, Oliver Goldsmith, and Oscar Wilde, all three poets and playwrights, and the philosopher George Berkeley.

A Literary Explosion

At the turn of the 20th century, Ireland experienced a literary explosion that gave the world some of its finest English-language literature and some of its most revered poets, playwrights, and novelists. Dramatists George Bernard Shaw, John Millington Synge, and Sean O'Casey, poet and playwright William Butler Yeats, and novelist James Joyce are just some of the important writers who burst onto the Irish literary scene in the early 20th century.

George Bernard Shaw (1856–1950) wrote more than 50 plays. Although Shaw lived in Ireland only until he was 20 years old, he always considered himself an Irishman. He once wrote, "I write as an Irishman

William Butler Yeats wrote about Irish life and traditions in his early poems.

. . . full of instinctive pity for those of my fellow creatures who are only English." In his plays, Shaw used his Irish wit to amuse audiences while driving home disturbing truths about humanity and society. His most famous plays include *Arms and the Man, Pygmalion, Saint Joan, Candida, Man and Superman,* and *Major Barbara.*

John Millington Synge (1871–1909) was born near Dublin and educated at Trinity College. He is best remembered for his plays about the farmers of the Aran Islands and their simple way of life, including *Riders to the Sea* and *The Well of the Saints,* and for his satires on contemporary Dublin society, such as *The Playboy of the Western World.* Along with his friend, the poet William Butler Yeats, Synge helped advance the idea that ordinary Irish people and their lives, rooted in centuries-old tradition, could be the subject of great literature.

Sean O'Casey (1880–1964), born John O'Casey in Dublin, was a patriot during the Troubles but later moved to Paris to write. His satiric plays, such as *Juno and the Paycock* and *The Plough and the Stars*, sharply criticized what he saw as the bigotry and hypocrisy of Irish society. He completed a six-volume autobiography in 1954.

William Butler Yeats (1865–1939) is recognized as one of the 20th century's finest poets. Yeats set out to become a poet early in life but did his most powerful work when he was in his fifties and sixties. His early poems are concerned mainly with Irish life and traditions; for example, in "The Lake Isle of Innisfree," written in 1892, Yeats celebrates the simple life of the Irish farmer. In his later poems, Yeats became more concerned with culture and events beyond Ireland; his powerful poem "The Second Coming" illustrates these concerns.

Sean O'Casey criticized some aspects of Irish society in his dramas.

Yeats, Shaw, Synge and the earlier Irish writers were from upper-class Protestant Anglo-Irish families. Before the turn of the 20th century, poverty and class discrimination excluded most Irish Catholics from the creative arts. But the rise of novelist James Joyce (1882–1941) from a poor Catholic family to literary greatness is a striking example of genius overcoming difficult beginnings. As one critic put it, Joyce was "like a rose blooming from an ash heap."

Today, James Joyce is considered one of the 20th century's most inventive writers. His books were banned in Ireland and other countries and widely condemned as obscene and even unreadable, but today they are read in many high schools and universities. They include *The Dubliners* (a collection of short stories) and the novels *A Portrait of the Artist as a Young Man, Ulysses,* and *Finnegan's Wake.*

The Irish people are proud of James Joyce. As one critic wrote, "Joyce traces the language to its source, where the spoken word and thought are

James Joyce introduced new writing techniques in his stories and novels. Most of them are set in Dublin or other Irish locations.

intimately bound together. With Joyce, language is not the vehicle and means of thought. It is the thought itself."

Ireland is no longer the center of literature that it was when Joyce, Yeats, and Shaw were writing. Later writers, including Frank O'Connor, Sean O'Faolain, and the playwrights Samuel Beckett and Brendan Behan, kept the Irish literary tradition alive for a time, but in recent years no new Irish writers have burst onto the scene with the same impact. Still, the Irish love of language endures.

The Mansion House has been the residence of the Lord Mayor of Dublin since 1715.

Dublin and Other Cities

Historically, Ireland has been a land of farms and villages. The ancient Celts lived in small settlements; later Viking outposts were no more than fortified towns. Not until the Normans came to Ireland in the 12th century did cities appear on the island. Even today, Ireland's cities are smaller than those of most other industrialized nations. Yet they are as full of history and culture as any in Europe.

The Republic of Ireland's capital and largest city is Dublin, with a population of slightly under 1 million (including its suburbs). Located on a natural harbor at the mouth of the River Liffey, Dublin is only 60 miles (96 kilometers) across the Irish Sea from Great Britain. This closeness to England has had a huge impact on the development of the city's unique character.

For 700 years, Dublin was the seat of English power in Ireland. It was also the site of many of the most dramatic episodes in the Republic of Ireland's long struggle for freedom. Robert Emmet's Nationalists staged their coup attempt here in 1803. In 1881, Charles Stewart Parnell, the "uncrowned king of Ireland," was imprisoned in Kilmainham Jail in Dublin on suspicion of inciting a farmers' revolt. The O'Connell Bridge, named after Daniel O'Connell, one of Ireland's most revered patriots, still bears bullet holes from the 1916 Easter Rebellion. After 1922, when Dublin became the capital of the Irish Free State, the influence of the English gradually declined. But even now, the city bears their stamp. Although it is now more Irish than it once was, Dublin remains more English than any other area of the republic.

Dublin dates back to ancient times. About 2,000 years ago, the Celts established a settlement where the River Liffey empties into the Irish Sea. They called the settlement Baile Atha Cliath, meaning "the place of the hurdle ford." The geographer and astronomer Ptolemy identified the settlement as "Eblana" on a map he made about A.D. 140. According to legend, Saint Patrick visited the settlement in the 5th century to convert the pagan Irish to Christianity.

In the 9th century, seafaring Vikings, led by Olaf the White, made their way to Ireland's east coast. At the mouth of the Liffey, they discovered the Celtic settlement. They also found a safe harbor, which they named Dubh Linn, meaning "the dark river pool." On a hill at the river's south bank they built a garrison that they used as a base for raids into the island's interior. Gradually, under Olaf and his successor, Ivarr the Boneless, the outpost developed into a major port and trading center, dealing in wine, cloth, and other goods.

Eventually, some of the original Viking invaders (called Danes by the Irish) mingled with the native Irish people and adopted Christianity. But more Vikings kept arriving on the island, and their predatory raids increased. Finally, in 1014, Irish high king Brian Boru led his army against the Vikings in Dublin. Although Brian Boru was killed in the fighting, known as the Battle of Clontarf, the Irish army defeated the Vikings and drove them from Dublin.

Barely a century and a half after the Vikings were defeated, Dublin fell to another set of invaders—the Anglo-Normans. In 1171, the English king Henry II visited Dublin and granted it to a group of Anglo-Norman settlers from Bristol, England. The settlers wasted no time in establishing Dublin as the center of Anglo-Norman superiority in Ireland. They built the stronghold of Dublin Castle within the small Viking city, rebuilt the walls of the Viking fortresses, and began to construct fine stone buildings to replace the Vikings' wooden houses and storerooms.

At this point, the history of Dublin began to depart from that of the rest of Ireland. While descendants of Celts and Vikings populated the countryside and carried on with their traditional ways of life, Dublin became primarily an English city, the point from which English settlers embarked to colonize other parts of the island. Until the late 16th century, English influence in Ireland was largely confined to a strip of land along the east coast, running from a little south of Dublin to the town of Dundalk, 50 miles (80 kilometers) to the north. This area was known as the Pale, or "the obedient shires." In the 17th and 18th centuries, English settlers gradually spread outward from the Pale into Ireland's interior.

A class of wealthy English Protestants based in Dublin, known as the Anglo-Irish or the Protestant Ascendancy, became the landlords of Ireland. Although many Anglo-Irish owned great farms and estates, most chose to live in the city and hired foremen to manage their holdings. During this period, Dublin reached a level of prosperity undreamed of before. Exports of meat, dairy products, and linen increased dramatically, and the city grew rich off the surrounding countryside.

By the end of the 18th century, Dublin was the second-largest city in the British Empire (London, of course, was largest). During this prosperous period, Dublin acquired most of its wide streets, splendid squares and parks, and majestic public buildings. Building projects were controlled by a committee fittingly known as the Wide Streets Commissioners. They gave the center of the city a spaciousness and a style that remain today. They improved the harbor to hold larger ships and reclaimed low-lying marshland to provide more space for building.

The handsome new buildings, many of which still stand, were adorned with ornate sculptures, plaster castings, wood carvings, and other decorative elements. The architecture and decoration of this period are usually referred to as Georgian, after the four English kings named George who reigned between 1714 and 1830.

Anglo-Irish landlords and merchants were not the only ones to flock to Dublin during this time. Many poor farmers, driven off their land by rising rents, came in search of jobs. But because the population of Dublin had increased fourfold in the years between 1700 and 1800, there were not nearly enough jobs to go around. Poverty and slums were the inevitable result. Hidden behind a glittering Georgian facade, Dublin's overcrowded and filthy slums were as bad as any in Europe. Epidemics of infectious diseases such as typhus swept through regularly, killing thousands. In some sections of the city, cemetery plots were so scarce that corpses awaiting burial piled up in the streets, exposing more people to infection. By 1900, more than half of the city's 300,000 inhabitants lived in deplorable conditions in the slums.

Fortunately, Dublin has a long history of social programs and institutions to help the poor and disadvantaged (although these programs too often fall short of their goals). In the 18th century, a concern for poor mothers-to-be moved a man named Bartholomew Mosse to found the Rotunda, the first maternity hospital ever built in Ireland or Great Britain.

Other institutions were supported by charity events; for example, in 1742, German-born composer George Frederick Handel conducted the first performance of his *Messiah* at the Charitable Society's music hall in Dublin. The Congregation of Religious Sisters of Charity, better known as the Irish Sisters of Charity, was founded by Mary Aikenhead in 1815. It was the first religious organization in Ireland formed mainly to aid the poor, and it founded Ireland's first Catholic hospital, Saint Vincent's, in 1834. Today, the Sisters of Charity continue to play a major role in aiding Dublin's poor. They run 18 primary schools and 10 secondary schools and performing a variety of services for the sick, the aged, and the alcohol-addicted.

In the 19th century, Dublin began to fall from fashion, although it continued to grow in size. Wealthy people and the new middle class of business and professional people fled the center of the old city for fashionable new developments in the suburbs, while famine-stricken rural people

Because of the city's leisurely pace and old-fashioned charm, shopping in Dublin is a great pleasure.

kept streaming into the city. By the thousands, these poor people moved into the once-magnificent Georgian houses and hastened their decay into slums.

The establishment of the Irish Free State in 1922 brought Dublin back to the forefront once again, as the city became the new state's capital. Trade and industry made a comeback, and the poverty and decay slowly receded. Today, the old Georgian buildings mingle with modern concrete, steel, and glass structures. Although some slums still exist, they are neither as numerous nor as delapidated as they once were, and even the worst are likely to have electricity and running water.

Dublin has continued to grow in the 20th century. Although it spans an area of some 45 square miles (117 sq km), the city retains much of its 18th-century charm and intimacy. Despite a recent building boom, no skyscrapers disrupt the gentle flow of its skyline. Indeed, visitors arriving by boat often remark how small and serene the city appears on the approach from the sea, nestled in its snug harbor between gently rolling hills.

Several rivers and canals, once used for transporting goods inland from Dublin's harbors, still trace their ways through the city. The largest is the River Liffey, which flows right through the heart of Dublin, cutting it almost in half. People may travel between the northern and southern halves by crossing one of the ten bridges that span the Liffey. Some of these bridges carry only pedestrian traffic; others, like O'Connell Bridge—Dublin's largest—handle tens of thousands of motor vehicles a day.

An abundance of public parks offers Dublin's people quiet, green havens from the bustle of city life. As a 19th-century historian noted, "No city in Europe is supplied with more extensive, more beautiful public squares, or so great a number of them, in proportion to its extent, than Dublin."

Dublin is also renowned for its historical buildings. The Republic's lawmakers meet in Leister House, a large building that dates from the 18th century. Other fine examples of 18th-century Georgian architecture include the Custom House and the Four Courts along the banks of the River Liffey.

Churches are another important part of Dublin's architectural landscape. Indeed, it is impossible to walk very far in any direction without coming upon a church. Christ Church Cathedral, the oldest building in Dublin, dates back to 1038. It was built by Vikings on the site where Saint Patrick is said to have preached in the 5th century. Later, the Vikings built Saint Michan's Church on the north side of the River Liffey. Saint Patrick's Cathedral was built around 1225, on the site where Saint Patrick himself is said to have caused water to spring from the earth by striking the ground with his staff.

Dublin is also the site of Ireland's most famous educational institution, Trinity College. Founded by Queen Elizabeth in 1591, Trinity was established to educate the sons of Protestant English aristocrats living in Ireland, and to help in "the reformation of the barbarism of this rude people [the Irish]." Today, it has a coeducational student body and accepts students of all religions.

The Library, Trinity's most famous building, was completed in 1732. More than 270 feet (81 meters) long, it has Ireland's largest collection of books and historical data, including the famous Book of Kells. It also contains Ireland's national symbol, a harp that is said to have belonged to Brian Boru, the high king of 11th-century Ireland (although this claim may not be accurate). Over the centuries, many famous writers attended Trinity, including Jonathan Swift, Oscar Wilde, Edmund Burke, and John Millington Synge. Besides Trinity College, Dublin is also the home of a branch of the National University of Ireland.

Many other Irish historical and artistic treasures are kept in Dublin's museums. The National Museum contains many fine examples of ancient Celtic art, including the Tara Brooch and the Ardagh Chalice. Both of these pieces, made of gold and silver, are more than 1,200 years old. The National Museum also has an extensive collection of glasswork, silver ornaments, and other elegant works from the Georgian period.

The National Gallery is Ireland's largest repository of paintings and sculpture. Besides works by Irish artists, such as Jack Butler Yeats (brother of poet and dramatist William Butler Yeats), it has an outstanding collection of paintings by European masters, including Rembrandt, Titian, El Greco, and Rubens.

Dublin is justly renowned as the cradle of Ireland's greatest playwrights and actors. Its most famous playhouse, the Abbey Theatre, was founded by Lady Gregory and William Butler Yeats at the beginning of the 20th century. Although it was destroyed by a fire in 1951, the Abbey has been rebuilt and gives regular performances.

The National Center for Culture and the Arts contains many fine examples of ancient Celtic art.

By far the most important industrial city in the Republic of Ireland, Dublin is home to more than one-third of the nation's manufacturing plants. Products include cloth and clothing, furniture, machinery, metals, foods, chemicals, paper, whiskey, and Irish stout, a dark, strong beer. Many of Ireland's export goods pass through Dublin's seaport before beginning their journey to ports around the world.

Cork

The Republic of Ireland's second largest city, with about 150,000 inhabitants, Cork is located near the Atlantic Ocean on the island's southern tip. The city's name comes from the Gaelic word *corcaigh*, which refers to the marshy island in the River Lee on which the city was once confined. Now the city extends far over the hills north and south of the river.

Cork was founded by Saint Finnabar in the early 7th century. Finnabar—who, according to legend, killed Ireland's last dragon—built a church and school on the island. But these and the other churches, abbeys, castles, and fortifications of past centuries have long since vanished. Today, Cork's oldest buildings date back only a few hundred years. One of the most beautiful of these, Shandon Church, has been immortalized in traditional Irish verse:

> Wherever I wander
> And thus grow fonder
> Sweet Cork, of thee
> With thy bells of Shandon
> That sound so grand on
> The pleasant waters of
> The River Lee.

Cork is Ireland's second largest manufacturing center. Some of the country's most important industries, including automobile manufacturing, shipbuilding, textile manufacturing, and oil refining, are located in or near the city. Its harbor, one of the best natural harbors in Europe, is an important shipping center.

Historically one of Ireland's most wealthy areas, Cork is also an important artistic and cultural center. A branch of the National University of Ireland is located there, and cultural events such as ballet, theater, art exhibits, and concerts are available. An international film festival is held in Cork every year, attracting film artists and fans from all over the world.

During the long years of English rule, Cork acquired the nickname "Rebel Cork" because it was the center of many Irish patriot activities. Among the many Cork patriots who died in the struggle for independence from England were two of its mayors, Thomas MacCurtain and Terence MacSwiney.

A few miles from Cork is one of Ireland's most popular tourist attractions—the Blarney Stone, in the 15th-century Blarney Castle. According to legend, Lord Blarney once saved his castle by persuading an attacking army to leave it alone. ("This is all Blarney; what he says he never means," Queen Elizabeth I of England is said to have complained about the lord of the castle.) Anyone who kisses the Blarney Stone—a feat

The City of Cork is Ireland's second-largest city and a manufacturing center.

that can be accomplished only by hanging upside down with another person providing support—is supposed to receive the gift of persuasion.

Farther down the River Lee from Cork lies the coastal seaport of Cobh, on Cork Bay. Once known as Queenstown, Cobh was called "the saddest spot in Ireland" by English writer H. V. Morton, because it was the main embarkation point for Irish people leaving the island for North America and other foreign lands. Cobh no longer handles emigrants; today, it is an important fishing town and the site of a naval base and a shipyard.

Limerick

Located on the banks of the River Shannon, Ireland's major river, is Limerick, the country's third-largest city. This port city is growing rapidly. In 1981, its population was just over 75,000, a figure that is expected to double within the next 20 years.

Limerick was founded by the Vikings in about A.D. 900, and it still bears traces of its Nordic origin (for example, a salmon fishery near the town still goes by its Scandinavian name of Lax Weir). But Viking power in the area was brought to an end by Brian Boru, and even after the arrival of the Anglo-Normans, Brian's descendants retained control of the city. In the 12th century one of those descendants, Donal Mor O'Brian, built a cathedral and a royal palace. The cathedral, which has been restored and enlarged, is now one of Limerick's principal points of interest. Another is the site on which Kincora, Brian Boru's castle, once stood. The castle has long since vanished without a trace, but many people visit the area nevertheless.

During the 17th century, Limerick suffered through several attacks and sieges, first by Oliver Cromwell and his troops and later by the forces of King William. In the 18th century, the city was rebuilt with wide streets and rows of brick Georgian houses.

Like Dublin and Cork, Limerick is an important manufacturing center and seaport. Food and clothing are its main products, and ships laden with Irish goods embark from the port to sail down the River Shannon and into the Atlantic Ocean for points overseas. Near Limerick lies Ireland's largest airport, Shannon, which handles flights from all over the world.

Galway

The small city of Galway, located in western Ireland on Galway Bay, is the fourth-largest city, with a population of just under 42,000 people. As the center of Gaelic customs and language, Galway is now considered the most Irish of all Ireland's cities. But this was not always the case. Galway was founded in the 13th century by Anglo-Norman settlers who held strict control over it for more than 400 years. The settlers would have nothing to do with the native Irish and in 1518 even passed a decree declaring that "neither O' nor Mac shall strut nor swagger through the streets of Galway." During this period Galway traded with Spain, and a man from Galway is said to have sailed with Columbus to America.

Today, Galway is a thriving university city, home to a branch of the National University of Ireland. It is also a popular vacation spot. Tourists can enjoy boating, fishing, swimming, and a popular horse race during the summer. Many also visit the nearby castles, including Portuna Castle, Dungory Castle, and Aughnanure Castle.

Waterford

Located at the mouth of the River Suir on Ireland's southeastern coast, Waterford is a fishing center and a busy port. The Vikings founded Waterford in the early 11th century. Reginald's Tower, built by the Vikings in 1003 and later reconstructed by the Normans as part of their fortifications, still stands in the city. It is now a tourist center and museum.

Today, Waterford has a population of nearly 40,000 and is home to a number of industries. The most famous is the Waterford glassworks, which produces expensive, high-quality crystal that is prized the world over.

Members of the underground IRA (Irish Republican Army) escort the coffin of deceased hunger striker Bobby Sands to the church.

An Uneasy Freedom

As it prepares to enter its fifth decade as an independent republic, Ireland faces several serious problems. It is experiencing its worst economic crisis since independence. The economic growth enjoyed during the 1970s has sputtered to a halt, and the Irish economy has stagnated. Unemployment and inflation are high; the foreign debt is astronomical. Ireland's taxes are the highest in Europe and growing rapidly, and the number of people receiving welfare payments has tripled in the 1980s. An estimated 100,000 young people have left the country in recent years, seeking better opportunities elsewhere.

But as bad as they are, these economic woes are not the worst of Ireland's troubles. Ireland's most enduring problems lie in the area of politics—specifically, the split between Northern Ireland and the republic.

The roots of this split are centuries old, dating back to England's policy of "plantation" colonization in the 1500s and 1600s. During this period, Scottish Presbyterians settled on land taken from Irish Catholics in the northern province of Ulster. Unlike many other settlers transplanted to Ireland from Great Britain, the Scots remained loyal to England in the centuries that followed. While the Irish Catholics were fighting for independence, the Protestants consolidated their hold on the north. Catholics in the north were treated like second-class citizens, denied the most basic human rights, persecuted for their religious beliefs, and condemned to live in poverty. The north became a symbol of British domination over Ireland, and Irish patriots made it a guerrilla battleground.

The battle lines were drawn in 1922, with the agreement that ended the war between England and Ireland. This agreement granted self-government to the 26 southern counties and split off the six Protestant-dominated northern counties into a separate country, with a government that was loyal to and dependent on England. The Irish Republican Army (IRA), the most anti-England and the most violent of the rebel forces, disputed this agreement; it wanted the entire island to be joined as a united and independent Ireland. The IRA called the Irish leaders who signed the agreement traitors. It began a bloody civil war in the south that spread to the Catholic ghettos of the north as well.

The Irish Civil War lasted almost two years. When it was over, the IRA and other rebel forces had been defeated by those supporting the agreement. But despite the defeat, the IRA refused to stop struggling for a united Ireland.

The troubles have intensified over the last two decades. Starting in the 1960s, Catholics in Northern Ireland have waged a campaign to gain civil rights and to overturn laws that have kept them poor and powerless for centuries. What began as peaceful protests soon turned into bloody riots between Catholics (backed by the IRA) and Protestant organizations such as the Ulster Volunteer Force and the Ulster Defense Association. Since 1969, when England sent several army divisions to stop the fighting, more than 20,000 people have been killed or injured.

In November 1985, hopes for peace were raised by the Anglo-Irish Agreement. This agreement, signed by the governments of England and the Republic of Ireland, gives the republic a voice in Northern Ireland's affairs. In exchange, the republic recognizes England's long-term sovereignty over the north. But, like the earlier agreement of 1922, the Anglo-Irish Agreement has only inflamed the Catholic-Protestant struggle. Since its signing, incidents of violence have increased sharply. The British army remains on guard, and the IRA continues its guerrilla war of ambush, assassination, and bombing.

Despite all the talk and promises on both sides, Ireland remains a land divided, and the killing continues. But Ireland's long history of struggle has bred in its people a determination to survive. Although the Emerald Isle may never again be united, the people of the Republic of Ireland are determined to build a modern, prosperous nation.

St. Mary's Cathedral in Limerick is a 12th-century building. The western front has a fine doorway in a style called Romanesque (influenced by southern European architecture).

◄GLOSSARY►

Ard ri	The Celtic high king.
Celts	An ancient European tribe that came to Ireland before the time of Christ and established an enduring civilization; they were also known as Gaels.
Curragh	A small boat made of canvas stretched tightly over a wooden frame.
Dail Eireann	House of Deputies, one of Ireland's two houses of Parliament.
Fianna Fail	"Warriors of destiny," one of Ireland's major political parties.
Finn Gael	"The Gaelic people," Ireland's second-largest political party.
Gaelic	An ancient Celtic tongue that is Ireland's national language.
Gaeltacht	The Gaelic-speaking western region of Ireland.
Ogham	A primitive form of writing using simple strokes. It was used to make inscriptions on Stone Age monuments in Ireland.
Oireachtas	Ireland's Parliament, made up of the Dail Eireann and the Seanad Eireann.
Passage graves	Prehistoric stone tombs still found throughout the Irish countryside.
Peat	Compressed, partially decayed vegetation formed in bags. When dried, it is used for fuel.
Plantation	A method used by England to colonize Ireland in the 16th and 17th centuries. English settlers were

"planted" on Irish land and the Irish farmers were evicted.

Ri A Celtic king, the ruler of a *tuath*.

Seanad Eireann The Senate, one of Ireland's two houses of Parliament.

Sinn Fein Society founded in 1905 to advance complete cultural and political independence from Great Britain. Gaelic for "ourselves alone."

Slean A special shovel used to cut blocks of peat.

Tuath A Celtic kingdom.

◄ I N D E X ►

U
Ulster Defense Association 120
Ulster Volunteer Force 120

V
Valera, Eamon de 93
Vikings 43–45, 108

W
Waterford 117
Wilde, Oscar 101, 113
wildlife 30
William of Orange 55

Y
Yeats, Jack Butler 113
Yeats, William Butler 100, 103